Living the Wisdom of Bhakti

Volume Two

Mahatma Das

Editing & Proofreading: Premāñjalī Devī Dāsī, Satyarūpa Devī Dāsī, Atrisha Ragoonanansingh, Bader Soma, Hugo Stetz, Nidhi Lakhiani, Matthew Sava, and Davina Parmar. Page & Cover Design: Gintare Ziedelyte. Layout: Nadine Lukesch. Cover photograph by Reddees, www.shutterstock.com. Photograph of Mahatma Das by Christina Alexandrova, 2017.

Library of Congress Cataloging-in-Publication Data

Das, Mahatma
Living the wisdom of bhakti

ISBN 979-8-3777-5229-5

1. Spirituality 2. Self-Development 3. Conduct of Life

Distributed by Sattva Books
Printed by Rathna Offset Printers, Chennai

To visit Mahatma Das on all his social media sites, to take his online courses, to subscribe to his WhatsApp group or receive his newsletters, please go to: Linktree at https://linktr.ee/mahat108

Also by Mahatma Das:
Japa Affirmations
Uplift Yourself, Change the World
Living the Wisdom of Bhakti Vol. 1

VOLUME TWO

LIVING *the* WISDOM *of* *Bhakti*

by Mahatma Das

SATTVA
BOOKS

Sattva Books
Alachua, FL, USA

To my spiritual master, His Divine Grace A.C. Bhaktivedanta Swami Prabhupāda. Without his blessings, I would never have been qualified to write any book on devotional service. I also dedicate this book to those who appreciate my work and to my godbrothers and godsisters who are always encouraging me to write books.

His Divine Grace A.C. Bhaktivedanta Swami Prabhupāda

Foreword

In 1974, on a morning walk in Paris, Śrīla Prabhupāda was asked, "What is the devotee's greatest enemy?" His startling reply was, "He himself, he's his greatest enemy. You become your friend. Nobody is enemy. You are yourself your enemy."

We see others doing something we consider inappropriate or ineffective and we want them to change. Yet, we're often reluctant or even resistant to make improvements in ourselves. We want others to change but the irony is we can only change ourselves.

Śrīla Prabhupāda created a clear and simple lifestyle of *bhakti*. We have learned what Prabhupāda has asked of us yet sometimes we find it difficult to apply in various circumstances.

Living the Wisdom of Bhakti addresses our unwillingness or lack of awareness by facilitating honest introspection. This journey of self-discovery encourages us to "get real" with ourselves.

From decades of experience in helping others, Mahatma Das expertly guides us in how to take a closer look at where we are and where we are going. He does this by encouraging us to ask questions of ourselves that are sometimes difficult to face but deeply rewarding to contemplate.

Philosophically and often humorously, Mahatma then assists us in our personal process of applying these self-discoveries in our daily lifestyles.

He addresses such important topics as:

- **letting go of resentment**
- **dealing with guilt**
- **resistance to change**
- **pretentious devotion**
- **the challenges of sexual purity**
- **cooperation strategies**
- **amending yourself instead of faulting others**
- **exploring your word of honor**
- **making your work a spiritual practice**
- **improving *japa***
- **seeing difficulties as mercy**

Living the Wisdom of Bhakti opened up my heart to exploring motivations and a new level of sincerity in my daily practice of Kṛṣṇa consciousness, especially in difficult situations. Reflecting upon all that I have read and studied in *Living the Wisdom*, I'm finding the application of simple honesty and perseverance to be deeply fulfilling.

Mahatma Prabhu has given us an intriguing set of exercises at the end of every chapter to help us in our personal journey of self-reflection. As a result, *Living the Wisdom of Bhakti* enhances a natural process so that positive changes can take place in our practice of self-realization.

Living the Wisdom of Bhakti is an exciting book to read and study; it's also a great book to share with others! Mahatma's suggestions on how to implement the transcendental knowledge that Prabhupāda has so kindly given us are empowering and joyful!

The numerous pearls of wisdom in this book are designed to help our devotional lives become what we visualize and pray for.

Have a simply wonderful journey,
Mahādevī Dāsī

Acknowledgements

I am deeply grateful to the readers of *Living the Wisdom of Bhakti – Volume One* for their encouragement to me to produce *Volume Two.*

I am also grateful to all the devotees who have attended my workshops and encouraged me by appreciating what they gained and sharing their realizations with me.

My godbrothers and godsisters, especially Indradyumna Swami, have been a great source of inspiration by pushing me to write books on the topics I teach in my workshops.

My family deserves special mention because this book would not have been possible had they not given me their loving support by allowing me the private time I needed to study, reflect and write.

Of course, it goes without saying that I couldn't have done anything without the mercy of my spiritual master, Śrīla Prabhupāda. His words and example are my life and soul and my reason for living. Without him I couldn't have written this book, nor would I have a reason to write any book.

Lastly, I would like to acknowledge devotees who helped in the creation and production of Volume Two. Except for a few of the later chapters, Premāñjalī Devī Dāsī, an English professor in Mauritius, did the editing by painstakingly making sure the text was easy to understand and relatable for all levels of devotees.

A team of editors and proofreaders led by my disciple, Satyarūpa Devī Dāsī from India, helped with the remaining chapters.

Nadine Lukesch from Germany did the layout and production, including the e-book version.

Gintare from Lithuania did the cover design with input from Prāṇadā Devī Dāsī.

Introduction

We are often good at knowing what to do, but bad at doing it. *Living the Wisdom of Bhakti* confronts this problem head-on.

This book doesn't focus just on learning something; its main focus is on becoming something. Sure, you will find verses, quotations, and stories from scriptures here. And you will learn new things. But knowledge is not power. It's the implementation of knowledge that is power. So my purpose is to help you better live the teachings of *bhakti*.

If you read this book, reflect, and do the exercises it recommends, you will find it easier to do what you may not be doing that you know you should be doing. You will also find it easier to change your life in general, to make it the way it should be, not the way it happens to be.

This is a workbook; a seminar on paper. *Volume Two* continues the self-exploration done in *Volume One* with an additional 38 chapters divided into six sections. Each chapter encourages you to look deeper into your mind and heart to find your inspiration as well as to identify the obstacles on your path. And many chapters contain exercises that will help you put the knowledge you are gaining into practice. This book is not passive. It's not meant to just be interesting or informative. *Living the Wisdom of Bhakti* is meant to improve the way you practice and live Kṛṣṇa consciousness.

Writing this book has helped me tremendously and I pray it will do the same for you. It has helped me because I have dared to challenge myself, dared to look deeper at my faith, commitment, desire, attachment, beliefs, vows, obstacles, anarthas, problems, relationships, *japa*, work, income, family, and my life in general – and then ask myself, "Is this how a Kṛṣṇa conscious person supposed to live?" In short, I dared to look deeper at what goes on both externally in my life as well as what goes on at a level I have been afraid to view in a totally open and honest way for most of my devotional career.

This book will challenge you to do the same.

When I decided to more deeply put into practice Śrīla Prabhupāda's teachings, I realized how theoretical my understanding of Kṛṣṇa consciousness was. As I tried to live Kṛṣṇa consciousness more genuinely, I saw more clearly how much I wasn't living it. My writing looks at this reality based on my own practice. As one devotee told me, don't teach it if you don't follow it. I didn't write about it unless I was the guinea pig.

I invite you on the journey to take your Kṛṣṇa consciousness deeper, become more real, genuine, introspective, honest, and above all fixed in your devotion to guru and Kṛṣṇa. I invite you to take a deeper look at where you are at and the great potential you have.

I invite you to do what's right, to make your life and your Kṛṣṇa consciousness the way you know it should be, the way you really want it to be. I invite you to do what you know you should do.

PS: For those of you who haven't yet read *Volume One*, you can scan the QR code given below to order the book on Amazon.com.

SCAN ME

How to Use This Book

I teach a workshop on forgiveness, but my workshop is not about forgiveness; it is about how to forgive. I help participants to acknowledge, confront and let go of their resentment.

In the same way, this book is not about Kṛṣṇa consciousness; it is about living Kṛṣṇa consciousness. In *Living the Wisdom of Bhakti* I address problems that all practitioners of Kṛṣṇa consciousness eventually face, and ask my readers to reflect on how these problems affect their lives. I analyze problems with the intention of shedding deeper light into the nature and depth of the difficulty and predicament we face. I then suggest practical solutions, solutions that are sometimes hidden between the lines of *śāstra*.

The rubber hits the road in the exercises found in each chapter because the exercises bring the teachings home. Each exercise helps you reflect on your personal situation, and offers ways to deal with your specific problems. The exercises help you (sometimes even force you) to put the teachings into practice. I do this to make this book as alive, interactive and practical as possible.

You can do the exercises as often as you like. Because the book is designed to relate to you at any stage of your Kṛṣṇa consciousness, the exercises remain relevant to you as you advance. Thus, you will gain new insight and realization as you use the book again in the future.

This is a workbook, a workshop, if you will, on paper. It is purposely designed to be thought provoking and self-exploring, and contains material that I have found to be extremely helpful for myself as well as for others. It is a result addressing the most common problems devotees face from a solution oriented approach, and takes into consideration the fundamental conditioning responsible for most of the problems we face. As such, it is recommended that you go over the material several times, reflect deeply upon it, digest it, and finally apply it.

My hope is the knowledge and exercises will help you overcome difficult problems, and move you forward in your Kṛṣṇa consciousness, your relationships, and in your life, with greater ease and success.

Table of Contents

Dedication v

Foreword vii

Acknowledgements xi

Introduction xiii

How to Use This Book xvii

Section One – ***Determination and Conditioning***

1. No One Can Help You Like You Can 25

2. Life Support 37

3. The Cause of The Problem 43

4. What's on Your List 49

5. Your Internal Alarm Clock 59

*Section Two – **Surrender to Kṛṣṇa or Drown in Māyā***

1. What to Pray For and How Kṛṣṇa Reciprocates *71*

2. Surrender to Surrender *79*

3. What Is Guru (Part One) *91*

4. What Is Guru (Part Two) *107*

5. What Is Guru (Part Three) *115*

*Section Three – **Creating Balance in Your Life***

1. Integration – Balancing Opposites *127*

2. Balancing Dependence and Independence *133*

3. The Balance Between Effort and Mercy *145*

4. Balancing Feelings of Unworthiness *159*

5. Balancing Taste and Sense Gratification *171*

6. Just Do It *181*

*Section Four – **Mini Japa Course***

1. Building Your Foundation *201*

2. The Importance of *Japa* in the Practice of *Bhakti* *205*

3. Your *Japa* Blueprint *209*

4. How Physiology Affects the Mind *213*

5. Be Present *217*

6. Sacred Space *221*

7. Entering Into the Mood and Meaning of the Mantra *225*

8. Chanting Is a Relationship *229*

9. Aligning Your Life With the Holy Names *233*

10. Bringing It Home *237*

*Section Five – **How to Make a Marriage Work***

1. Why Marriages Don't Last *243*

2. Husband As Guru *257*

3. A Happy Wife Has a Good Husband *269*

*Section Six – **Spiritual Self-Development***

1. How to Change This Year: You Need to Freak Out *287*

2. Don't Die With Your Music in You *293*

3. Humility Means Happy Small *299*

4. What Is the Problem *307*

5. Taking Responsibility Is Liberating *315*

6. Reasons We Blame or Criticize Others *319*

7. The Position of Guilt in Spiritual Life *333*

8. Is Forgiveness Possible Before We Are Pure *337*

9. Self-Compassion *341*

About the Author *351*

SECTION ONE

Determination and Conditioning

CHAPTER 1

No One Can Help You Like You Can

You may be wondering why I chose "No One Can Help You Like You Can" as the title for this chapter. This statement comes from a conversation in which a devotee asked Prabhupāda for help, saying that he was not able to follow the four rules. Prabhupāda looked sternly at him and said, "If you do not follow the regulative principles, then no one can help you."

Following the practices of Kṛṣṇa consciousness is the platform from which help comes. It is not that we attract mercy by virtue of the fact that we are so fallen that we can't follow or don't try to follow. To think this way only perpetuates the problem. Devotees feel in great need of mercy, not because they are having difficulty following principles or vows, but because they don't feel they are spiritually advanced and thus need help.

Prabhupāda put great stock in the power of making vows, teaching that taking one's vows seriously was foundational to spiritual progress. Of course, we can pray to Kṛṣṇa that we keep our vows, but the point is to keep them no matter what, and to not expect that by some magical stroke of mercy, we will be able to do it. The mercy and magic is in the instructions of the spiritual master and we get this mercy by following those instructions.

Backwards Thinking

"Backwards Thinking" means to think "I need to be spiritually strong in order to follow my vows," when in fact our strength and determination come as a by-product of our commitment to the promises we make. It is the same as saying "I need to have energy before I can exercise" when the fact is that energy comes as a by-product of exercise.

When Prabhupāda was asked how we may become determined to follow the regulative principles, he saw in that question a major defect. Asking how to keep a promise – which is what asking how to get the determination to follow our vows means – indicated to Prabhupāda a lack of commitment, because one who is committed wouldn't ask this question.

The above situation is synonymous to the following scenario. I borrow money from you and pay you back monthly. But, then I stop paying you and call you and ask, "How can I become more determined to pay you back?" If someone said that to you, you would reply exactly as Prabhupāda did by saying, "You promised. A gentleman keeps his promise. Why did you promise if you didn't plan to pay me back?"

Kṛṣṇa says in the *Bhagavad-gītā* (18.35): "And that determination which cannot go beyond dreaming, fearfulness, lamentation, moroseness and illusion – such unintelligent determination, O son of Pṛthā, is in the mode of darkness." One in the mode of ignorance has virtually no choice. Their will is totally asleep. Don't allow your will to go to sleep. And if it's gone to sleep, wake it up. Remember, if you make no choice, that's also a choice.

"99% a Problem, 100% a Breeze"

"99% a problem, 100% a Breeze" means that if you are not 100% committed, even 1% doubt about following your vow leaves you open to not committing and thus makes it that much more difficult to keep your promise. Prabhupāda explains that when you make a commitment to fast, you can fast without much difficulty. That's because you have not allowed yourself a way out. But if you leave yourself open to the slight possibility that you won't fast, then you make it difficult on yourself to keep the fast.

Would you have an open-heart surgery if the surgeon said he or she is 99% committed? Would you marry if your spouse were less than 100% committed to the marriage?

There's a difference between interest and commitment. When you are interested in doing something, you do it only when it's convenient or easy. When you are committed, you accept no excuses, only results.

In life, it's the people who are 100% committed to their outcomes who are really successful. It's such a simple concept but so many people wake up every day and fight with themselves over whether or not to keep their commitments, stick to their disciplines, or carry out their plans.

The "No Exceptions" Rule

Successful people make a "No Exceptions" rule. Once you make a 100% commitment to something, there are no exceptions. Once you commit 100% to your spouse – that's it. You don't have to think about it again. You don't have to wrestle with the decision every day. You burn the bridges, and this makes life simpler. For example, if you don't feel like finishing your rounds, not finishing your rounds is no longer an alternative if you follow the "No Exceptions" rule. So that solves the problem. The bridges are burned. You are going to finish your rounds. You already decided long ago that there would be no excuses for not finishing your rounds.

Disempowering Beliefs

The number one thing that is holding us down in anything we attempt is the lack of belief in ourselves. One of the reasons we find it difficult to commit is that we think we can't do what we committed to do. If you don't think you can do it, you are right – you can't do it. The phrase "I can't" is the most powerful force of negation in the human psyche. Tell a child they are not good at something long enough and even if they are good at it, they will never succeed because they have been convinced otherwise. That is because the image of ourselves is so powerful that we can't do anything that goes against that image.

In *Living the Wisdom of Bhakti*, Volume 1 (Section Two, Chapter 3: Your Beliefs Affect Every Area of Your Life), we told the story of a man whose friends played a trick on him and convinced him that he had died and become a ghost.

Prabhupāda tells the story in a morning walk in Los Angeles (September 28, 1972) as follows. So there was a circle of friends. All the friends conspired to make another friend bewildered. So they conspired that, "As soon as you meet that gentleman you cry, 'Oh, here is a ghost! Here is a ghost! Here is a ghost!' So all the friends, they come, 'Oh! You are dead, you are ghost, you are ghost!'" So after ten times like that, he thought, "Have I become a ghost?" Then he became bewildered, "Whether really I have become ghost, I am dead?"

How many times a week do you tell yourself, "I can't follow that principle because I am too weak," or "It's really difficult for me to follow this practice because I am not a disciplined person," or worse, "I don't think it's possible for me to be Kṛṣṇa conscious in this life?" And then you blame your inability to not follow on being weak, undisciplined, or even on the process of Kṛṣṇa consciousness itself (by telling yourself it is a difficult process). We understand that Kṛṣṇa can work through us to do the impossible. Do you think that if every person that you met told you that you are a spiritual person, that you are a person of integrity, that you have great potential to make spiritual advancement, it would influence the way you follow your devotional practices? You can also tell yourself those same things. Or you can tell yourself the opposite. But whatever you tell yourself, that is what is most likely to happen because your mind doesn't distinguish between what's real and what isn't. So you could be well equipped to be Kṛṣṇa conscious, but if you constantly tell yourself you are not, you make it difficult for yourself to be Kṛṣṇa conscious. If we view ourselves as a failure, we tend to fail.

Look at your excuses and you'll find your beliefs. Also, look at how you behave and you'll find your beliefs. Ask yourself, "What would someone who is doing what I do, thinking what I think, or saying what I say, believe?" Any beliefs you discover that go against your ideals are obstacles to your success.

Aim Higher

"The greatest danger for most of us is not that we aim too high and we miss it, but we aim too low and we reach it." *(Michelangelo)*

Most people think too small, aim too low, and quit too soon. Why? They don't believe in themselves. I am sure you know someone who is qualified to be successful but isn't, because they think they are not qualified. And those who think this way become so insecure that they will only do things that they are sure will succeed; otherwise they would be crushed by failure. So isn't it true that we are made more by the choices that we make than by our personal qualifications?

Without belief in ourselves, we'll always aim lower than what's possible for us. We'll be frightened to move out of our comfort zones. And unfortunately, for some of us, being very Kṛṣṇa conscious is out of our comfort zone. It's not that we can't be Kṛṣṇa conscious; it's that we think we can't be.

Rūpa Gosvāmī prays to the Lord: "I have no qualifications to be Kṛṣṇa conscious but I have great hope that I will become Kṛṣṇa conscious because you are the friend of the most fallen." Rūpa Gosvāmī was looking at his hope, not his disqualification. You never see that disqualification holds the pure devotee down. That's because Kṛṣṇa is more interested in our hopes than our disqualifications. Kṛṣṇa will empower us to achieve what we want, despite all our disqualification. In fact, the disqualifications actually bring more of His compassion upon us because the more disqualified we are, the more we need His mercy. Knowing this, we can set our aspirations high: "I am so fallen that Kṛṣṇa will help me more."

The key to following our vows is to set our aspirations much higher than the vows. For example, if a couple's primary aspiration is to remain married, it may end up becoming difficult to stay together, what to speak of having a good marriage. Rather, if their goal is to have a wonderful Kṛṣṇa conscious marriage and relationship, staying together is simply a natural by-product of this goal.

Prabhupāda said that if you try for first class, you'll get second class. And if you try for second class, you'll get last class. In Kṛṣṇa consciousness our goal is not to chant 16 rounds a day and follow our vows. Our goal is to become completely Kṛṣṇa conscious. We want to enter into an eternal loving relationship with Kṛṣṇa, to be reinstated in our eternal *rāsa*. We all have a place waiting for us with Kṛṣṇa. Our service, our name, what we look like, how we dress, our age, our family – that is already waiting for us. That is meant to be our highest aspiration. And simultaneously, we aspire to bring everyone else there with us. If that's what we aspire for, then chanting 16 rounds and following the principles will not be very difficult.

Sooner or later, we will get what we expect. Usually, the people who keep failing are the ones who expect to. If you ask any devotees who are doing well in their spiritual lives what their aspirations are, you will generally find that their aspirations are much higher than just being a strict follower of principles.

Manage Your Decisions Daily

Many of us run into difficulty when we think, "I've made a commitment and that's all there is to do about it." But the choices we make don't stay chosen by themselves. The key is to manage our decisions and choices daily. For example, since we are meant to follow Kṛṣṇa conscious principles daily, every day we have to arrange our lives in such a way that we can do that. It's not enough to have made the commitment a year ago; we have to make that commitment daily – and practically manage that decision.

Good decisions, good commitments, and good choices don't automatically stay good. What if we are having a bad day? Do we write it off and say, "Well, I didn't chant well today, or I didn't chant all my rounds because I was having a really bad day?" No. We deal with the bad day so we can still follow our commitments and chant good rounds.

Failure

"A man is not defeated by his opponents but by himself." (Jan Smuts)

What are the chances of making a commitment and at some point failing to keep it for some time? If you take a vow and follow it throughout your life without fail, in today's world you will be quite special. I don't want you to think that it's okay to fail, that you should expect to fail, or that you should expect to break a promise. My point is that if it does happen, then the most important thing for you is to know what to do after you fall so that you continue to make spiritual advancement without letting the fall deter your enthusiasm and determination.

There's a big difference between failing and being a failure. We are conditioned. Prabhupāda said that it's not unusual for one practicing spiritual life to fall victim to the allurements of wealth, women and money. And he said that Kṛṣṇa would forgive us for accidental fall-downs. So an accidental fall-down is sometimes unavoidable. But after a fall, staying down is not unavoidable. In fact, when you have the right attitude, you can actually use failure to your advantage.

When devotees fall, they often become discouraged and depressed. When someone in this condition comes to me, I ask the devotee, "What's good about your fall?" Their normal response is nothing is good about this. But I keep asking and the devotee realizes all the mistakes they made that lead to that fall. Then I ask, "So what did you learn from this?" And we try to review the lessons in a way that ensures, as far as possible, that it won't happen again. And usually the devotee realizes that they would never have learned the lessons they needed without the fall (part of the lesson they learn is that they are not as Kṛṣṇa conscious as they thought they were). Then I ask, "If the result of this fall is that you have understood enough about yourself and falling down so that it's less likely to happen again and so that you may be able to maintain your vows for life from this point on, then was falling a good thing? Was falling necessary for you?" And they see the sense in that and their entire attitude changes.

The truth is that sometimes the only way to learn something is to fail. Maybe we think we can play with *Māyā*. If we do, we will have to get burnt a little to learn the lesson that we can't mess around with her. Sometimes we learn much more from our failures than from our successes, hence the saying, "sometimes you win and sometimes you learn." The reality is that we will make mistakes on our way to success. Once we accept this, we can remain positive despite our failures.

The alternative to this is to feel guilty and discouraged. And this leads to more guilt, which leads to more discouragement, which leads to more guilt, which leads to – you guessed it – more discouragement. It becomes a vicious cycle. The point is that if I fall, I can get up with even greater determination and enthusiasm. What holds us down is when we say, "if only I had not done this or that." Then we just live in the past and lament, which are all signs of ignorance. You can't change the past, but you can change the future by the way you act and react in the present.

What we should say is, "next time I will do this or that." That is determination in goodness. And if you do better next time, then the past wasn't a failure. It was just a learning experience, and this is how you should refer to it.

Kṛṣṇa explains in the *Bhagavad-gītā* (18.33): "O son of Pṛthā, that determination which is unbreakable, which is sustained with steadfastness by yoga practice, and which thus controls the activities of the mind, life and senses is determination in the mode of goodness."

This verse should be cited to describe a determined person after they fall, not only one who never falls. Maybe we can't immediately climb back to the same heights we were at before, but we should at least be standing and moving upwards. And some will aspire for even greater heights after a fall. We are not finished when we are defeated. Failure doesn't mean we'll never succeed; it just means it will take a little longer.

It's interesting to note how guilty we can make ourselves feel when we fail. But Prabhupāda encouraged every devotee, no matter how fallen, to come back to devotional service. He never made them feel guilty. He always welcomed them with open arms. Devotional service is the solution to the problem. We can't solve the problem by running away from service.

Laziness can hold us down after a fall. It is said that laziness is the secret ingredient of failure but it's only kept a secret from the person who fails. To be Kṛṣṇa conscious, we must refuse to quit. Whenever I've had difficulty, I always understood that this was the optimum time for *māyā* to discourage me. So I would usually react by becoming twice as enthusiastic. You may wonder how I could do so after failing. The truth is that you can become twice as enthusiastic any time you want. It doesn't matter what happened a minute ago.

Thanks for reading these principles and I hope they will help you better follow your vows and resolutions.

CHAPTER 2

Life Support

Analyze your daily activities in relation to vows you have taken by determining if the way you live supports or undermines your vows. For example, do you ever feel that the way you live, act, or think makes it difficult to keep some of your vows? If so, these are red flags that you need to heed.

The Ramification of Saṁskāras and the Environment on Our Vows

Prabhupāda describes a *mahātmā* as one who will not allow himself to be in a situation that doesn't support the realizations he needs to remain in Kṛṣṇa consciousness.

"Now, in the conditioned state, sometimes devotional service and the conditional service in relation to the body will parallel one another. But then again, sometimes these activities become opposed to one another. As far as possible, a devotee is very cautious so that he does not do anything that could disrupt his wholesome condition. He knows that perfection in his activities depends on his progressive realization of Kṛṣṇa consciousness." (*Bhagavad-gītā* 9.30, Purport)

Prabhupāda tells us that to properly follow our vows we must live a lifestyle that gives us the realization and strength needed to continue following those vows. You must focus on all the activities you need to do (or avoid) and the environment you need to create that will support your vows. And if we are not doing this, it likely indicates that we are not taking our vows seriously enough (or that we don't realize how much our environment affects us). All your actions create *saṁskāras*, mental impressions or mental dispositions. Thus whatever you do, say, see, eat, etc. affects your consciousness. As you ponder this, you become more aware of the correlation between what you are doing and how you are thinking and feeling. You may have sometimes experienced a lack of interest or taste for chanting or *sādhana*. If so, it's likely related to what you have been recently doing or not doing such as what you have been saying, eating, hearing, etc.

How to Change Saṁskāras

How can you alter behavior that is difficult to change, such as habitual behavior? *Saṁskāras* are powerfully created by what we see. So when you see someone with qualities you would like to possess, or when you see someone acting in a way you would like to act, it creates mental impressions on you, and you begin to desire to be or act like that person. Even hearing about being or acting in a particular way is powerful.

When an impression is made in your consciousness, it tends to produce an inclination to think in a certain way and thus act in a certain way. As those thoughts and actions are repeated (we tend to have the same thoughts daily), it makes a deeper impression, thus causing further repetition of that action. Of course, if the action is desirable, that is good. If it's not desirable, it forms an unwanted addiction.

Consider the vows you wish to better follow or wish to make and then determine how your life would need to change in order to support those vows. Can you make those changes? Can you maintain those changes? Answering these questions will better help you determine how ready you are to follow those vows.

So two questions bear considering – why make vows to begin with, and what is it about yourself that prevents you from fully embracing the vows you have taken? In Buddhist philosophy for example, vows are taken to create merit. That merit isn't present without taking a vow to engage or refrain from a certain behavior. Not killing is the right thing to do, but taking a vow not to kill and enthusiastically holding that vow, creates a karmic impetus that elevates the consciousness of the practitioner in a way that simply refraining from the behavior alone cannot accomplish. Similarly, in Twelve Step programs, the decision made in step three is to wholeheartedly engage in working on steps four through twelve in order to have a spiritual awakening. As step twelve states, "Having had a spiritual awakening as THE RESULT of these steps, we tried to carry this message to (alcoholics) and to practice these principles in all our affairs." To create positive karmic results, there has to be a tangible form of commitment that goes beyond mere sentiment. Step Four in the Big Book of Alcoholics Anonymous says, "Made a searching and fearless moral inventory of ourselves." Step Five continues, "Admitted to God, to ourselves, and to another human being the exact nature of our wrongs." Finally Step Ten declares, "Continued to take personal inventory and when we were wrong promptly admitted it." So how does all of this apply to strengthening broken or degraded vows or taking new vows in Kṛṣṇa consciousness? By integrating the scriptural, yet oftentimes, ignored tradition of confession into our lives, we can become renewed and restored vow holders and vow keepers.

Let's examine how this process can be put into practice for those of you who are having a tough time maintaining your vows. First, be honest with yourself about your condition. This is the hardest step for most people. The reason for this is usually guilt and shame. Guilt, if it takes on the quality of remorse, will be a motivating factor to be honest with your situation. However, by taking on the quality of shame, guilt becomes both a hindrance and an excuse to continue in the mode of ignorance due to the pain of facing the reality of what you have let yourself become. Remember that everything that is done in the dark will eventually come to the light. Fear is another stumbling block for most people – fear of failing ourselves, failing our guru, and failing Kṛṣṇa. The third and maybe the most detrimental defect preventing honesty is false pride. Remember that pride comes before a fall and we must humble ourselves before Lord Kṛṣṇa, who is the only true controller. Don't allow ego to keep you from Kṛṣṇa!

The next step is to seek out an experienced devotee to whom you can confess your shortcomings, one who can help you to see the reality of your situation while at the same time, offering compassion and assuring you of forgiveness and the chance for a return to the high road of keeping your vows and commitments. The things this devotee should be alert for is the presence of self-centered and self-seeking behavior on your part that you may not be clearly seeing, and should be firm and strict in their own commitments so that you may be helped, rather than enabled. The important thing to remember is that when you fall down from a higher consciousness, it is the same pitfalls that have been experienced by others in your situation that are responsible, so by owning up to them and listening to the feedback of an experienced senior devotee, you are taking a major step towards being proactive in your own return to the value system you freely chose when you took your vows. Be humble, open, honest, and receptive, and allow Lord Kṛṣṇa Caitanya's infinite mercy to pour into your heart and elevate you back into a position of true *bhakti*. Recall that you took those vows so your internal values could match up with your external actions, and rejoice that there is a mercy from the Lord that is as vast as an ocean.

Śrīla Prabhupāda said this about confession:

"Because we have lived so many years without being Kṛṣṇa conscious, we have lived only a sinful life, but Kṛṣṇa assures us that as soon as one surrenders to Him He immediately squares all accounts and puts an end to all one's sinful activities so that one may begin a new life. When we initiate disciples we therefore tell them, "Now the account is squared. Now don't commit sinful activities anymore."

One should not think that because the holy name of Kṛṣṇa can nullify sinful activities, one may commit a little sinful activity and chant Hare Kṛṣṇa to nullify it. That is the greatest offense (*nāmno balād yasya hi pāpa-buddhiḥ*). The members of some religious orders go to church and confess their sins, but then, they again commit the same sinful activities. What then is the value of their confession? One may confess, "My Lord, out of my ignorance I committed this sin," but one should not plan, "I shall commit sinful activities and then go to church and confess them, and then the sins will be nullified, and I can begin a new chapter of sinful life." Similarly, one should not knowingly take advantage of the chanting of the Hare Kṛṣṇa mantra to nullify sinful activities so that one may then begin sinful acts again. We should be very careful. Before taking initiation, one promises to have no illicit sex, no intoxicants, no gambling, and no meat-eating, and this vow one should strictly follow. Then one will be clean. If one keeps oneself clean in this way and always engages in devotional service, his life will be a success, and there will be no scarcity of anything he wants." (*Teachings of Queen Kuntī*, Chapter 23: Natural Prosperity)

CHAPTER 3

The Cause of the Problem

In this chapter we discuss how, in the attempt to control our mind, we often only deal with the effect, the thoughts, and not the cause of the thoughts. Thus the thoughts we try to control continually come into our minds. It requires looking more deeply into the nature of our consciousness.

Where Did That Thought Come From?

How can we control negative thoughts? We must control them at their source. Thoughts are the effect of a deeper cause. The cause may be envy, jealousy, a desire to possess, control, or enjoy something or someone, a fear, something we wish to hide from others, pride, hatred, or beliefs that no longer serve us.

To change our thoughts, it's essential to acknowledge that our thoughts, even the ones that are highly conditioned by past actions, have their roots in our own self-created soil. It may seem like they are coming from outside of us, but we must have the soil within us to nourish them. Otherwise, they will not take root. If, by chance, they do take root and we don't nourish them, they will die.

I Can't Control My Mind

Devotees often say, "I am having trouble with my mind," "My mind is difficult to control," "My mind is giving me trouble." Why blame our problems on our mind? Again, we must recognize that the cause of any trouble with the mind is self-created. Since thoughts are an effect, they reveal to us their cause. Change or root out the cause, and thoughts will change. This is Kṛṣṇa consciousness.

We can't control the mind unless we change the nature of our desire. Of course, we may be able to control the mind temporarily, just like we can temporarily control symptoms of a disease. However, if we don't eliminate the cause of the disease, the symptoms reappear.

Aligned With a Higher Purpose

The reason we have thoughts of envy, jealousy, pride, or hatred, is because we nurture these qualities. Why would we nurture them? We nurture them because we get something 'desirable' from them. For example, if we hate someone, we may be thinking that the hatred allows us to get back at them for the wrongs they have done to us. In this case hatred serves a purpose for us. At the same time it harms us. The irony is that we are the ones creating those thoughts. Our envy creates the hatred, and then we suffer from it and regret having those thoughts.

When we have thoughts we don't want or need, thoughts that don't serve our higher spiritual aspirations, we are out of alignment. Our spiritual self wants one thing, but our mind often works against us and we end up with thoughts that make it difficult or impossible to properly achieve our spiritual goals. The first step to dealing with this problem is to admit that we are allowing it to happen. Since we are the ones creating the problem, we can create the beliefs and desires that are in alignment with our highest needs, goals, and aspirations. When we align our desire with our spiritual purposes, Kṛṣṇa conscious thinking becomes natural and almost effortless.

Starving the Demon Within

Kṛṣṇa says to control the lower self by the higher self. One way I do this is by reminding myself what my higher self wants and that I don't want what my lower self really thinks it wants. When I find a conditioned response to a situation, I remind myself this is not what I want and this is not the way I want to respond; this is just my conditioned side acting up. I then reinforce to myself the way I prefer to respond. What this does is keep me in touch with my devotional side.

As Śrīla Prabhupāda says, the devotee and demon are in the same body. (Śrīla Prabhupāda Remembrances – Siddhānta dāsa, ITV – Chapter 34 – Jagat Caksu) We want to nourish the devotee to health and starve the demon to death.

Our Thoughts Affect Others

Not only do our conditioning and the state of our consciousness affect us, but they affect others as well. Thoughts have physical waves and these waves affect others. If we think positively or negatively about a person, it affects them. We can see this with kids and pets. If we love and appreciate them, they feel it. If we are upset with someone, even if we don't express the upset, they usually can feel it. If we expect or hope that someone will behave a certain way, either good or bad, our thoughts will affect them. This is why it is said a moment's association with a *sādhu* can change one's life. A *sādhu's* Kṛṣṇa conscious presence can deeply affect (and positively infect) our heart. This means that our Kṛṣṇa consciousness, or lack of Kṛṣṇa consciousness, will be experienced by others.

Elevating Others Begins at Home

We should work to raise the consciousness of the world, not only by the way we behave, but also by raising our own consciousness. When we go to a temple, we feel elevated and blissful because of the Kṛṣṇa consciousness of the other devotees in the temple. Imagine the effect that millions and millions of such devotees would have on the world. Prabhupāda said that if one percent of the world would become Kṛṣṇa conscious, then the whole world will change.

"So, there must be a portion of the population well versed in brahminical culture. *Ekaś candras tamo hanti na ca tara sahasrasaḥ*. Just like in a garden if there is one nice flower plant, rose, with good scent, the whole garden becomes flavored, you see? Scented. Similarly, we do not expect that the whole population of the human society will be taking to this brahminical culture; but even one percent of the whole population accepts this brahminical culture, Kṛṣṇa consciousness, then the whole world will be peaceful. Not even one percent, less than one percent. It is so nice." (Lecture in Los Angeles, December 4, 1968)

We are the only ones who can elevate the consciousness of the world. What we think today not only affects ourselves, but it also affects those in our world.

CHAPTER 4

What's on Your List

Someone once asked me, "What's the most important practice for advancing in spiritual life?" Śrīla Prabhupāda said chanting of Hare Kṛṣṇa is most important. Some have suggested that devotee association is more important because without it, most of us wouldn't have the strength to chant Hare Kṛṣṇa.

I agree. But I think there is a principle even more fundamental than this. I have addressed it to some degree in other chapters as well, but it warrants further discussion.

Our very desire to advance in spiritual life is the core condition upon which our advancement is built.

"One's devotion and sincere desire to serve the Supreme Personality of Godhead are the only qualifications. Rūpa Gosvāmī has also said that the price for achieving God's favor is simply one's sincere eagerness to have it (laulyam ekaṁ mūlyam)." (Śrīmad-Bhāgavatam 5.19.7, Purport)

Transcendental Greed

When people seriously take to spiritual life, they begin a process of extricating themselves from material activities, some of which they performed for their entire lives. And they start breaking bad habits they had for years. It's like they become a new person, a person that achieves levels of self-control and discipline that practically no one in the world follows. How are they able to do this? There is only one reason: somehow or other they sincerely want Kṛṣṇa consciousness above all other things.

It is this transcendental greed that is our lifeline to Kṛṣṇa consciousness.

So yes, association of the pure devotees and *sādhus* and chanting Hare Kṛṣṇa is the most important practice. But the point is that if a sufficient level of intensity to become Kṛṣṇa conscious is not there, no one would do the practice. Good food is healthy, but it's only healthy if you can digest it. Our eagerness to be Kṛṣṇa conscious is our digestive power.

"If one develops this *laulyam*, or excessive eagerness for meeting and serving the Lord in a particular way, that is the price to enter into the kingdom of God. Otherwise, there is no material calculation for the value of the ticket by which one can enter the kingdom of God. The only price for such entrance is this *laulyam lālasā-mayī*, or desire and great eagerness." (*Nectar of Devotion*, Chapter 9)

Get Your Will Out of the Bed

Go back to the time when you were first taking up Kṛṣṇa consciousness seriously. What were you thinking? How were your desires changing? Wasn't it almost like there was a bubble around you making it as if nothing could ultimately check your forward progress?

If it's not like that today, it's time to connect more deeply with that very sincerity, that driving force that first brought you to Kṛṣṇa, that eagerness. Don't think you have no control over this. That thinking is our enemy. We are advised to cultivate this kind of greed. This is what Kṛṣṇa consciousness is all about.

"Yes, Kṛṣṇa consciousness is available. You can purchase it from this Kṛṣṇa consciousness movement. But what is the price? It is such a nice thing, but you have to pay the price. What is that? *Tatra laulyam api mūlyam ekalaṁ* [*Śrī Caitanya-caritāmṛta, Madhya-līlā* 8.70]: Simply your eagerness. That is the price. You have to pay this price. Then you get Kṛṣṇa, immediately. Kṛṣṇa is not poor, and the Kṛṣṇa-seller – the Kṛṣṇa devotee – he's also not poor. He can distribute Kṛṣṇa free. And he's doing that. You simply have to purchase Him by your eagerness." (*Journey of Self Discovery*, Chapter 2)

If that greed is not there intensely, we can conclude that the lower modes of nature have covered it. Our will to be Kṛṣṇa conscious can go into a state of slumber. Have you ever been in a situation where your desire to be Kṛṣṇa conscious has weakened and you are left wondering where it has gone? It is there. You just need to strengthen it, or as this analogy goes, wake it up.

So what will it take to get the will out of bed and become fully active and intense? It will take one thing – you. And I think that is the one thing too many of us are afraid to admit. We breathe more easily when we think the will is weak because of........... and we make a long list of things. What's on your list? Here are some things that might be on it.

- I don't live near a temple
- I don't get a lot of good association
- Most of my time is spent at work
- I had a very sinful past
- I am not very .... (fill in the blanks)
- I am not the same now as when I first started practicing Kṛṣṇa consciousness
- I have to .... (fill in the blanks)
- My health is not good
- I have a bad temper
- I have a heavy mind
- I have difficulty controlling my senses
- I am weak around the opposite sex
- I watch too much TV
- I am addicted to pornography
- I have hobbies that I love that take a lot of time
- I don't have enough time for my spiritual practices
- My spouse isn't Kṛṣṇa conscious
- My spouse and I don't get along well

OK, I'll stop here before I take up the next 25 pages with valid reasons for not being as eager as we need to be to get Kṛṣṇa.

What's on your list? Take out a piece of paper and start writing down all the reasons that are preventing you from being more

Kṛṣṇa conscious, from being eager, from having *laulyam* for Kṛṣṇa. And when you look at your list, ask this question: Is it absolutely true that this is preventing me from being eager to be Kṛṣṇa conscious?

The resounding answer must be, "Of course it is not absolutely true that this is preventing me from being Kṛṣṇa conscious." If you really want Kṛṣṇa, nothing on that list would prevent you, just as nothing prevented you when you first decided you wanted to be a devotee. You could have had even a longer list when you were first coming to Kṛṣṇa. But you didn't. Why? Because you were eager for Kṛṣṇa. And that eagerness burns that list to pieces.

One of the most deceptive forms of *māyā* is to use Kṛṣṇa conscious philosophy to keep us away from Kṛṣṇa. This happens when we understand the words of scripture or of our gurus in a way that, unknown to us, are actually beliefs that keep us down in Kṛṣṇa consciousness. What can happen (and often does happen) is when we think we are reading and understanding scripture, we are really only reading our own mental script. For example, when we believe advancement is so dependent on the right association, getting blessings, receiving mercy, etc. we often allow our own will to be Kṛṣṇa conscious to take a secondary position. When one buys into this paradigm, one starts to fall prey to thinking they have little control over this and becomes more or less helpless. The point is that we do have control over this. The idea that "I can't" is one of *māyā's* most deadly weapons. It is not "can you," but rather "will you."

"My Mercy Is Already There"

Prabhupāda addressed this when one of his disciples prayed to him for his mercy and Prabhupāda replied, "My mercy is already there." The implication is that this devotee was not taking advantage of what was already given, what was already available, and thinking that advancement is something mystical, like a rain of mercy that automatically makes one Kṛṣṇa conscious. I have seen this subtle form of *māyā* come up so many times. Devotees think once I go here, get married, get this service, etc. I will be more Kṛṣṇa conscious. And although there is validity in this, the thinking that those situations in and of themselves will make one Kṛṣṇa conscious is a common misunderstanding and is often so subtle that we don't always realize how we are affected by it.

What also goes along with this thinking is the idea that as one advances in devotional service, one will automatically develop the qualities and traits necessary for being more Kṛṣṇa conscious. This is another way to disempower yourself. Instead of taking responsibility to cultivate spiritual qualities and practices, one will feel that all one can do is practice *sādhana* and everything else needed for becoming a pure devotee will automatically manifest. And when it doesn't, nothing more is done to work on oneself. The reality is that *bhakti* is the force that empowers us to be able to manifest spiritual qualities in our daily lives and adhere to spiritual practices, not a force that puts our will to sleep.

Focus on Where You Want to Go

Connecting with my Kṛṣṇa conscious desires helps me to be focused on where I want to go rather than where I don't want to go. More important than where we are now, is where we are looking to go. We progress by focusing on what we can do or where we want to go, not on what we can't do or why we don't like where we are at.

Meditate on how wonderful it will be when we get a little closer to being where we want to be. Imagining how you will feel when you get there is motivating. When I see a devotee with qualities and characteristics that I would like to possess, I think about how nice it would be to be like him or her.

When our actions are not aligned with our goals, we are allowing material nature to make decisions for us rather than deciding for ourselves. When we came to Kṛṣṇa consciousness, we declared war on *māyā*. We turned away from material life and we didn't allow material situations to influence our decision. We knew what we wanted and moved towards it.

This sincerity of purpose that brought us to Kṛṣṇa is what will continue to keep us in Kṛṣṇa consciousness. If we disconnect from this sincerity, we are weakening one of our most important lifelines to Kṛṣṇa.

Mental Impressions

There's a problem with not overcoming our conditioning that we may not be fully aware of. When we allow our conditioning to motivate our actions, the conditioning is reinforced. When we act in Kṛṣṇa consciousness, it reinforces our desire to serve Kṛṣṇa. So the problem with any action that is out of alignment with our goals is that it reinforces the desire to perform those actions. To counteract this, we must act in alignment with our goals, even when we don't feel like it. These actions will create the tendency to repeat themselves.

In Sanskrit, these are known as *saṁskāras*, tendencies or mental impressions. We commonly refer to these as habits.

Start It Yesterday

If you wait to feel like acting before doing something that's important, then that's not intelligent. You might end up waiting for a few thousand more lifetimes before you finally get around to doing it. You just need to act. When do you need to act? I hear you say, "Okay, I'll do it tomorrow." In America, when asked when we want something done, if we are in a rush we'll say, "I want it done by yesterday." So if you are hesitant in aligning your actions with your goals, I suggest you start on your new behavior yesterday.

The act in itself will later produce the feeling to act that way again. If a person who says I am too tired to exercise waits until he feels like exercising, he may never do it. But if he just does it, he'll feel better and eventually he will love doing it. The point is that often you are not able to think yourself into a new way of acting, but you can act your way into a new way of thinking.

Motivation is what gets you going. Habit is what keeps you going.

CHAPTER 5

Your Internal Alarm Clock

How much sleep is enough? How much is too much? Some of us may need a little more sleep and some of us may need a little less. But when we are more Kṛṣṇa conscious, we all need less sleep. At least we want to sleep less.

This chapter deals with these aspects in detail.

Śrīla Prabhupāda did not like to sleep. He felt that it was a waste of time. He once said: I am praying to Kṛṣṇa that I can live without eating and sleeping.

How did Prabhupāda write his books while developing and running a worldwide movement? He awoke after a few hours of sleep and worked on his books all night. Bhaktivinoda Ṭhākura did the same. He was able to write over 100 books while supporting a large family because he stayed up most of the night.

Successful people minimize their sleep in order to have more time. Yes, it's their passion that keeps them so active, but passion is better than ignorance. Once Prabhupāda found his servant and secretary sleeping for hours after lunch. He told them that they were worse than the *karmis*, because the *karmis* were working, but they were sleeping. (An excerpt from *Memories – Anecdotes of a Modern-Day Saint* by Siddhānta dāsa) Clearly, Prabhupāda did not want his disciples to sleep more than absolutely needed.

Prabhupāda told Tamala Kṛṣṇa Mahārāja that learning to sleep less requires practice. Of course, it also helps to go to bed early, because every hour of sleep before midnight is twice as more restful than those after midnight.

Our body gets energy from our mind. When I am inspired in Kṛṣṇa consciousness, I sleep less. A bored and frustrated person will generally sleep a lot more than needed. Please note that any difficulties with mental health may potentially affect sleep (e.g., sleep disturbances, sleeping too little or too much). Please seek professional help if there are any concerns with this.

We all have an internal alarm clock, so if we wish to sleep less, we'll need to reset our alarm. How do you sleep less if you know that you need a certain amount of sleep? Do you believe you need a certain amount of sleep because of your experience, or are you experiencing that you need a certain amount of sleep because you believe you need that amount? If you don't get the amount of sleep that you believe you need, do you automatically tell yourself you are tired (or must be tired)? "It's so early. Boy, am I tired." Of course, if you believe you need more sleep than you actually do, you probably don't believe that you are programmed to believe that.

Rising when you would like to get up is best done by setting your internal alarm clock. Of course, to program yourself to rise earlier, you need good reasons to be up that early. One of the best ways to give yourself these reasons is simply to start getting up earlier. Why? Because by doing this you experience the power of, and get a taste for, the early morning hours.

There are many devotees who are up every morning at 4 o'clock, 365 days a year. How do they do this? They have internalized this time so deeply within themselves that every day they easily and naturally rise by 4 am.

Early morning is the best time for chanting and study. Prabhupāda wanted his disciples to be awake by 4 am. If you are not rising this early, there is probably nothing as transformational for your spiritual practice as to rise at this time. Your chanting and reading will be much more powerful and effective at this time. Plus, you will have more time to hear, chant, do *pūjā*, etc. before your day starts. This will make a huge difference in your life.

It's all too easy to stay up late and rise just in time to eat and go to work without doing any spiritual practice before starting your day. This schedule undermines your spiritual life. The longer you do this, the more it becomes a habit. When you do this, you will struggle to find good time for quality chanting and reading. Thus, the quality of your *sādhana* will usually only be a fraction as good as it would have been if practiced in the morning.

I notice that the less Kṛṣṇa conscious I am, the more I tend to sleep. Eating, sleeping, mating and defending are grouped together. The more one advances in Kṛṣṇa consciousness, the more these activities are reduced. That's because these activities become less and less attractive as one advances.

If the mantra, "this is how much sleep I need," is really more sleep than you do need; then this is tied to your level of spiritual advancement, your internal commitment to your spiritual practices, your inspiration in Kṛṣṇa consciousness and a belief, conditioned by many factors, in how much sleep you need. But no matter how many hours you sleep, rise as early as possible.

Prabhupāda often talks about being engaged in Kṛṣṇa's service from four in the morning to ten at night. What is significant about four to ten? These are the hours when we take care of the Deities. Kṛṣṇa rises at 4 am and rests in the evening at around 9 pm. (After putting Kṛṣṇa to sleep, cleaning the *pūjārī* room, etc., the *pūjārī* will get to bed around 10 pm.)

You should make it your goal to be awake by four in the morning because Prabhupāda repeatedly told us that we should rise by four. Impregnate this instruction in your mind with the mantra, "rise by four." Here's a story that might help you do this.

Toṣaṇa-Kṛṣṇa took rest in another room, while Prabhupāda went on writing all night, his pen scratching on the hollow wooden desk. Then, at four in the morning, Prabhupāda rang the little bell Toṣaṇa-Kṛṣṇa had left with him and called, "Toṣaṇa-Kṛṣṇa" Toṣaṇa-Kṛṣṇa came running. "Yes, Prabhupāda?"

"It is four o'clock," Prabhupāda said. "You should get up." Toṣaṇa-Kṛṣṇa had run to the door without his glasses, so he hurried back to get them. He then ran back again to Prabhupāda's room and sat down before him. (*Prabhupāda-līlā*, Chapter 5, Satsvarūpa Dāsa Goswāmī)

If you just can't rise by four, at least you should be awake during *brāhma-muhūrta*, one and a half hours before sunrise.

One of the things that impressed me to maintain a schedule of early rising is the fact that many, many people are up at four or five in the morning meditating, doing yoga, exercising, running or walking. They are not necessarily up early just because it's a good time to exercise. Many are up early because they are busy people. If they don't rise early they won't find the time to exercise. I find it a paradox to be sleeping while non-devotees are already up and doing their own form of "*sādhana*."

We are also supposed to be up that early. In a lecture Prabhupāda simply says, "...according to the Vedic system, everyone should rise early in the morning before four o'clock." (*Śrīmad-Bhāgavatam* lecture 1.1.5-6, London, August 23, 1971)

Prabhupāda explains, "We can observe that in demoniac societies, the dark, late hours of night are considered most appropriate for recreational activity. When a demon hears that someone is rising at four o'clock in the morning to take advantage of the godly early-morning hours, he is astonished and bewildered." (*Śrīmad-Bhāgavatam* 11.2.49, Purport)

In Māyāpur, we see about three hundred pilgrims lining up at 4 am to get in the temple. Their culture is that when going on pilgrimage you attend *maṅgala-ārātrika*.

"At four o'clock, attend the *ārātrika*, *maṅgala-ārātrika*. *Maṅgala-ārātrika* means auspicious beginning of your day." (Lecture on *Nectar of Devotion*, November 13, 1972)

How important is rising early? Girirāj Swami talks about his experience with Śrīla Prabhupāda at the Kumbha-melā.

"The program was very rigorous, because it was bitterly cold at night and we were expected to get up at four o'clock in the morning and bathe and attend *maṅgala-ārātrika*. So a few staunch devotees like Tamala Kṛṣṇa got up early – by three or three-thirty – and walked all the way from our camp to the Gaṅgā to take an early-morning bath. But those of us staying in the *brahmacārī* tent were not so staunch, and generally when it was time to get up at four o'clock, it was so cold out that we preferred to remain in our sleeping bags.

Śrīla Prabhupāda also started to notice that some of us were coming late to *maṅgala-ārātrika* and that some of us were not coming at all. Prabhupāda became very upset about this, because he knew how important *maṅgala-ārātrika* was for us. So one morning, although he was a little frail in health, he got up at four o 'clock and came out in his *gamsha*, sat down under the pump, and took that ice-cold bath early in the morning – just to encourage us to get up, bathe, and come to *maṅgala-ārātrika*. That had a very profound effect on all of us, and we felt so ashamed that we just couldn't sleep late anymore."

When anyone asks me, "How can I make spiritual progress?" my answer is always, "Get up early." I don't say this only because Śrīla Prabhupāda stressed rising early. My personal experience is that even though I may be inclined to stay up late, one of the best things I can do for my spiritual life is to rise early.

What if we come alive at night and find it difficult to go to bed early. What if we naturally stay up late? This question not only relates to sleep, it relates to any practice in Kṛṣṇa consciousness that seems to go against our nature.

We engage our nature in service. We don't want to deny or repress our natural inclination and inspiration for service. But it's different with *sādhana*. If we wish to make steady advancement in Kṛṣṇa consciousness, a certain amount of *sādhana* is a must, whether or not we find it natural or easy.

Of course, there are choices in *sādhana*. I may like to read but am less inclined to *pūjā*. I may like to chant and do *pūjā* more than I like to read. That's fine. But, there are five main activities to *sādhana bhakti* (chanting, hearing, associating, worshiping the Deity, and living in a holy place) that are most important. When done together they have a synergistic effect.

So when it comes to *sādhana*, the mantra must be, "We do it even if we don't feel like it."

If we are not rising early, how do we make the transition to become early risers? Inspiration is important. But inspiration doesn't necessarily translate into continued action. Inspiration is often a fleeting enthusiasm. We might hear or read something that motivates us to improve our life, and for a few weeks we are inspired to continue our new way of thinking and acting. Unfortunately, it's common to gradually lose the motivation to continue the practice.

When inspiration doesn't last, it is likely that, that motivation was predominately another's enthusiasm, understanding and realization, not our own. However, when it becomes something that we really want to do, no one has to inspire us. We inspire ourselves.

Sādhana means practice and *sādhya* means the goal of the practice. *Sādhana* is motivated by rules and regulations and *sādhya* is motivated by one's own desire to engage in devotional practice. In *sādhana* one thinks, "I have to chant my rounds." In the *sādhya* stage one thinks, "I want to chant my rounds. I get to chant my rounds." In *sādhana*, sixteen rounds may be a struggle. On the *sādhya* platform, it's difficult to stop at sixteen rounds.

By the repeated practice of *sādhana*, done properly, a natural desire to perform that activity gradually awakens. Yet, we still need motivation to keep us going in the *sādhana* stage. So how do we avoid going from initial inspiration to apathy?

Perhaps you are getting inspired to rise earlier by reading this chapter. Whether or not you make this desire your own will determine whether or not the inspiration translates into a regular practice.

Prabhupāda explains this in a lecture. *Guru-mukha-padma-vākya, cittetekoriyāaikya*: "Make the orders of the spiritual master your life and soul." And then, *ārnā koriho mane āśā*: "Do not think otherwise." Simply accept what he says.

It doesn't mean that you initially need to develop an attraction for an activity to make it your own. Of course, in the long run the attraction must be there for you to maintain a regular practice. But, you can make it your own long before the natural attraction develops.

Why does a devotee do anything on a daily basis that's not easy for him? It's because the instruction to do it becomes, as Prabhupāda said, "Your life and soul." The important question here is, "How do we make an instruction our life and soul?"

I doubt there is one answer for all of us. But I do know that it's an important question to ask ourselves.

Let's look at possible answers to the question, "How do we make a spiritual practice ours?"

1. We may adopt a spiritual practice that we don't naturally like doing knowing that eventually we will develop an attraction for that activity.
2. We strongly believe in the value of the practice, and wish to adopt values in our life that will inspire the practice.
3. We understand (or bring ourselves to understand) the vital importance of the practice, causing us to make the activity a priority in our lives.
4. We envision the positive results of the practice and the negative consequences of living without it.

Of course, if we can follow Narottama dāsa Ṭhākura's advice of "Simply accept what he says," we can alter our lifestyle immediately in accord with the instructions of our guru. Then, simply because Prabhupāda said to rise by four in the morning, we do it. This is the platform that we should all aspire to reach. Whatever is my guru's desire becomes my own desire.

"From four in the morning until ten at night (from *maṅgala-ārātrika* to *śayana-ārātrika*) there must be at least five or six *brāhmaṇas* to take care of the Deity. Six *ārātrikas* are performed in the temple and food is frequently offered to the Deity and the *prasādam* distributed. This is the method of worshiping the Deity according to the rules and regulations set by predecessors." (*Śrī Caitanya-caritāmṛta, Madhya-līlā* 4.87, Purport)

"Everything is done in conformity to a regular standard. For example, all the temple members, without exception must rise by 4:00 am and attend *maṅgala-ārātrika*. Everyone living in the temple must agree to the standard by proper understanding of the philosophy of *tapasya*. We cannot expect our guests to follow all our principles, but whoever lives in the temple must follow." (January 12, 1974, Letter to Mukunda Dāsa)

Is rising early an instruction just for temple devotees? I believe it's one of our most important practices, whether or not you live in a temple.

SECTION TWO

Surrender to Kṛṣṇa or Drown in Maya

CHAPTER 1

What to Pray for and How Kṛṣṇa Reciprocates

Śrīla Bhaktisiddhānta Sarasvatī Ṭhākura used to pace back and forth on his balcony and pose questions to himself, and then answer them. I do the same in this chapter.

I ask the questions to myself and then answer them. I ask subtle questions that I believe are important for our progress in Kṛṣṇa consciousness.

I ask about the nature of pure prayer: Is it wrong to pray to Kṛṣṇa to protect us materially? Is it okay to pray to Kṛṣṇa to fulfill material desires that would help us in devotional service, or make us more peaceful so we can be more steady? And would such prayers indicate a lack of faith in His protection and maintenance?

I also ask if praying can change our karma. If praying is wrong when we don't endeavor to achieve what we are praying for, do we really need to pray if we are already making a full effort to achieve our goals (what we are praying for), and if Kṛṣṇa knows everything, do we really need to pray to Him at all?

Since we all have our individual karma, if we are praying to Kṛṣṇa to attain something that we are not destined to get according to our karma, can we still get it?

Yes, praying can change our karma. But since karma is Kṛṣṇa's law to bring us closer to Him, why would He change it? There is a verse in *Bhakti Sandharba* that says if we only approach Kṛṣṇa for material things, Kṛṣṇa will reciprocate with that foolish person; but he won't get *bhakti*. For this reason our mood should not be to ask for material things unless such material things or desires are in relation to Kṛṣṇa's service.

Kṛṣṇa uses our karma to purify us, so if we pray to change that karma we may be praying to Kṛṣṇa to interfere with His plan for what is best for us. But normally, whatever our karma, Kṛṣṇa reduces the reactions for us.

Śrīla Prabhupāda said it may be our karma to have our head cut off, but because we are devotees, we only get a cut on our finger. As a devotee becomes purified, he no longer needs purification of his full karma, so it is reduced by Kṛṣṇa. Also, no matter what kinds of happiness and distress await a devotee, by responding to them in a Kṛṣṇa conscious way, a devotee is less affected by the happiness and distress. This is one way our destiny changes by surrendering to Kṛṣṇa, i.e. we see and respond differently to our karma. Plus, we experience greater happiness in devotional service than what our karma can ever bring us.

Being disturbed by happiness and distress is an impediment to *bhakti*, so if we tolerate them we will be spiritually happy. And by advancement in Kṛṣṇa consciousness we learn to better tolerate happiness and distress. Ultimately, our desire to pray for something material is about being happy. And by Kṛṣṇa consciousness we can become many times happier.

Kṛṣṇa will either reduce our karma or utilize it for our spiritual advancement. Receiving Kṛṣṇas protection means that Kṛṣṇa does what's best. Usually our karma is what's best for us, so Kṛṣṇa uses it.

The main thing is to always pray in a way that invokes our dormant love.

How would you answer the above question in relation to devotees who are mostly engaged with work and family? Is there a difference between how karma affects them and how it affects those who are "fully engaged" in service?

The whole meaning of God is that He reciprocates with His devotees. So it depends on the devotee's attitude, not *āśrama* or external situation. If one's *āśrama* affects their spirit of dedication, then it will affect how Kṛṣṇa reciprocates ("*ye yathā māṁ prapadyante*").

Since every desire we have is known to Kṛṣṇa, and every desire is really a prayer, is there any difference in the result we obtain by desiring something that we don't pray for and desiring something we do pray for?

The desire itself is the essence of prayer, but prayer is one of the processes of devotional service. So we should pray. Also, praying intensifies the desire. And from the position of *rasa*, not everything is known to Kṛṣṇa; He is forgetful if that serves the *rasa*. So it's best to both desire and pray because maybe He won't fulfill a specific desire unless we pray for it.

If my desire is material, since Kṛṣṇa already knows what it is, why bother Him by asking Him to fulfill it? Plus, wouldn't this show a lack of faith and purity since Prabhupāda says, "A pure devotee of the Lord is ashamed to ask anything in self-interest. but householders are sometimes obliged to ask favors being bound by the tie of family affection."

In distress a devotee will want to seek shelter someplace; so why not seek help from Kṛṣṇa? That seeking shelter is a natural flavor of love because the servant's mood of love is that Kṛṣṇa is my maintainer and protector. Of course with that confidence one may consider that there is no need to ask anything from Kṛṣṇa because He is already maintaining and protecting us. So according to our faith we will ask – or not ask – Kṛṣṇa for help. But either way there should be a mood of devotion, i.e. whatever we pray for, even if it is material, should help our *bhakti* in some way. Still, what we ask for will often depend on our level of faith.

Is there some way to purify what may seem to be a materially-oriented prayer, by praying for it, only if I think it will help my service? In this way, although I may pray for a spouse, material security, or health, my mood is that with these things I can better serve Kṛṣṇa and if He desires to give me these things I will use them for Him?

Yes, if you need to pray and compromise the spirit of love by asking God for something, then try to acknowledge that God's will is best and what pleases Him most is by asking, as you have suggested, for things that will enhance your service, not your sense gratification. And if you are not sure if what you are asking for is proper, you can add the phrase "if you so desire" to your prayer.

It seems unproductive, perhaps even useless, to pray for something that we don't strongly desire and thus don't actively pursue. For example, I could pray to become free of envy but do little or nothing to become non-envious. To me this is like asking someone to help me carry a table, and they lift their end, and I don't lift mine. There is a saying, "Act like everything depends on you and pray like everything depends on God." So is it improper to pray unless we are willing to make efforts to achieve what we are praying for?

I don't think it is useless to pray this way because a devotee's mood is that everything depends on Kṛṣṇa. It is an acknowledgment that we are not independent of Him, which is the mood of surrender and the gateway to *bhakti*. So we ask for purity and at the same time, the act of praying itself is the consciousness and endeavor for purity. In other words, praying for something that we do not yet strongly desire, and are thus not really pursuing, is still purifying as an act of *sādhana*, and by acting in this way the pure desire can develop. We can also pray for the desire to want to become pure.

If we have a strong desire for pure devotional service, and thus take care to perform the activities that will help us achieve this, won't that get us to our goal even if we don't pray to achieve it? In other words, if I am totally fixed on my goal, isn't that really the perfection of prayer, the external manifestation of prayer. Or is prayer still necessary?

Prayer is still necessary to keep us in the humble mood of dependence on Kṛṣṇa to achieve success. Otherwise our determination may turn to into *ahaṅkāra*, thinking that I can achieve everything by my own power.

What about prayers to help us out of dangerous situations? A devotee doesn't ask Kṛṣṇa for anything. Yet at the same time is totally dependent on Kṛṣṇa for protection. In danger, we pray to Lord Nṛsiṁhadeva. Draupadi prayed to Kṛṣṇa to protect her and Uttarā came to Kṛṣṇa when she saw the brahmāstra coming. Only Kṛṣṇa can protect us, so is it wrong or right to seek and ask for protection? Or should we just ask Kṛṣṇa to protect our devotional service?

In *Nectar of Devotion*, Śrīla Prabhupāda says we should go to the Lord and reveal our troubles to Him. Prabhupāda also said go to Gaura Nitāi, tell Them your problems, and They will do the needful. Again, if protection is motivated ultimately by the desire to be pure, then such prayers are welcome. Sometimes we circumstantially have to ask Kṛṣṇa for material help because He is our only shelter and we are in great difficulty. And the nature of such prayers and dependence will reflect the level of our advancement.

So although we want to elevate the quality of our prayers to not have to ask Kṛṣṇa for anything on our own account, we also want to be real when we pray.

It seems there is a fine line between accepting a situation and praying to change a situation. When we pray for changing a situation that we can personally do nothing to alter, we may be putting ourselves into a mindset in which we will be unable to deal with the consequences if the situation doesn't change. Is there a guideline?

Sometimes we need to pray for the strength to deal with the situation rather than pray to change the situation. "Kṛṣṇa, please give me the strength, intelligence, and ability to deal with the challenges that I face."

What about the prayers of one who asks the Lord to save him from the ocean of birth and death? Can we say that on the platform of vaidhi, this is appropriate, but on higher platforms of bhakti it is not? And how does this relate to the question about praying to Kṛṣṇa for protection?

For a neophyte, a prayer to be saved from the ocean of birth and death is in accordance with his level of advancement. He is suffering in the material world and wants to get out. This suffering is a strong impetus for him to be Kṛṣṇa conscious. For a more advanced devotee, he wants to be free from the ocean of birth and death in the sense of, "Place me as an atom at your lotus feet." He always wants to serve the Lord, free from all material impurities, be it in heaven or hell.

CHAPTER 2

Surrender to Surrender

The word itself doesn't bode well with many of us. The word surrender evokes fears of losing freedom, of losing control, even of losing individual identity. Surrender can bring up connotations of 'forced acceptance'.

For many of us, the first image that comes to mind when we hear of 'surrender' is that of the battle weary soldier giving himself over to his enemies. We may picture ourselves as those soldiers, helplessly clinging to our attachments as they are torn away from us. Certainly, if this is surrender; who wants it? However, this is not surrender; this is fear of surrender. Surrender is sweet. Surrender is voluntary. Surrender is what happens when we love. The holy name urges us to surrender – even begs us to surrender. But when we are afraid to heed its call, our japa *suffers. There is a part of us that fears that the holy name will bring us too quickly to the ocean of surrender, an ocean that may be colder or rougher than we think we can handle. In this case, we prefer to walk in the water slowly and gradually – and our* japa *reflects this mood.*

One of my friends confided to me that he would get caught in cycles of surrender and retreat. The more he tried to surrender, the more the path became full of rocks and choked with thorns; the hardships grew stronger. He realized that if he fully surrendered, he would have to make changes to his life that he feared he just could not maintain. So even as he hears the sweet, holy name calling him to surrender, fear of that ocean of surrender keeps its grip on his soul. In this chapter, we look at the subtle aspects of our resistance to surrender and how this affects our bhakti in general and our japa in particular.

For many of us the word surrender bears negative connotations. We fear that if we fully surrender to Kṛṣṇa then something "undesirable" may happen.

- "If I fully surrender, what if Kṛṣṇa takes away something I am attached to?"
- "If I fully surrender, what if Kṛṣṇa won't allow me to do my favorite services?"
- "If I fully surrender, what if Kṛṣṇa makes my life more difficult?"
- "If I fully surrender, what if I won't be happy?"

Śrīmad-Bhāgavatam states that one who reads or hears this great book will always be absorbed in thoughts of Kṛṣṇa. In the *Bhakti-Sandarbha*, Jīva Gosvāmī poses the following question: "Why doesn't this happen when we hear the *Śrīmad-Bhāgavatam*?" He explains that it doesn't happen because we don't want to fully surrender. In other words, we deprive ourselves of the full benefit of the *Bhāgavatam* (and the other processes of *bhakti*) because of our reluctance to surrender. Do you want to get closer to Kṛṣṇa? I am sure that you do. But are you thinking, "Yes, I want to get closer to Kṛṣṇa, as long as I don't have to fully surrender, because I may not like the way Kṛṣṇa brings me closer to Him?" Or maybe you are thinking, "Yes, I would like to surrender fully to Kṛṣṇa, but not just yet." "I don't mind if Kṛṣṇa takes away this attachment, but I don't want Him to take away that attachment." Kṛṣṇa wants a relationship with us. If He didn't care about us, He wouldn't have appeared in His various incarnations and He wouldn't have sent so many pure devotees to this planet to try to deliver us. What is missing in the relationship is our reciprocation of His love for us. For so many lives, we have taken from Kṛṣṇa; now it's our turn to give back.

What will Kṛṣṇa do if we fully surrender to Him? Will He make our lives difficult? Will He take things away from us? Will He give us services that are full of difficulties, or that go against our nature? He may or may not do these things. But we should have faith that if we surrender to Kṛṣṇa, He will only deal with us in a way that brings us closer to Him.

Acts of surrender bring us into a more intimate relationship with Kṛṣṇa. So we can say that one meaning of surrender is, "that which brings us closer to Kṛṣṇa." Yet on some level, perhaps a level we are not fully conscious of, many of us are actually afraid of having a closer relationship with Kṛṣṇa.

Good relationships develop when we are willing to make sacrifices and compromises, we are responsible and trustworthy, we act with integrity, we are true to our word, we reciprocate with the love given, and love even when our lover is unkind.

How well does Kṛṣṇa do this for us? Perfectly well.

How well do we do this for Kṛṣṇa?

How often do you devote more energy to fulfill your own desires than you do to fulfill Kṛṣṇa's desires? How often do you forget to be grateful for Kṛṣṇa's gifts to you? How often do you fail to remember Kṛṣṇa during your day?

As conditioned souls, we have a reluctance to allow Kṛṣṇa to fully take control of our lives. In a *Vyāsa-pūjā* address to his spiritual master, Śrīla Prabhupāda described this as "causeless unwillingness" to serve. Causeless unwillingness means behavior motivated by a long standing desire to avoid Kṛṣṇa.

Satsvarūpa Mahārāja once asked Śrīla Prabhupāda: "Why, if Kṛṣṇa is so attractive, is it so difficult to surrender to Him?" Prabhupāda replied, "Because you hate Kṛṣṇa."

Do we really hate Kṛṣṇa? It doesn't seem like it. We serve Him, we glorify Him, we pray to Him, we chant His name. These are not the activities of one who hates Kṛṣṇa. So what did Prabhupāda mean?

Even though we serve Kṛṣṇa, the tendency to want to be like Him is still strong. In many ways we still want to enjoy like Kṛṣṇa. We want to enjoy the opposite sex; we want to enjoy some honor, power, control or opulence. Granted, these desires may be fairly well subdued, but this means that in some way we are still trying to play out God's role. In other words, we are often competing with Kṛṣṇa in various ways, some subtle and some not so subtle. Although we might not think of these tendencies or actions as manifestations of hatred towards Kṛṣṇa, at least we can admit they are not expressions of love for Him. So what are they?

We want to love Kṛṣṇa and this is why we practice Kṛṣṇa consciousness. But our conditioned nature is still afraid to fully love Him. Love entails giving our heart, losing our independence, and subordinating ourselves to the one we love. Love means our lover is first in our lives. Love is a sacrifice and love of God is the supreme sacrifice. Divine love means we are controlled solely by Kṛṣṇa's will. Indeed, divine love is far more than simply reciprocating with Kṛṣṇa's love. It is divine slavery. It's such a high level of self-sacrifice that even Kṛṣṇa cannot repay this love. Surrender is full of sweetness, but in our conditioned state we tend to look at surrender differently. We often fail to see how total surrender can make us happy and how it will fulfill our desires. So we monitor our surrender by being cautious about what we are willing and not willing to sacrifice to guru and Kṛṣṇa.

If you sat before Kṛṣṇa, would you feel guilty or awkward about your inability to properly reciprocate with His love? If you sometimes do things that have little or nothing to do with Him, or are even in direct opposition to what He asks of you, how would you feel with having to admit this to Him?

Each of us must confront our fears about surrender (about coming closer to Kṛṣṇa). After all, the goal of Kṛṣṇa consciousness is to repair our broken relationship with Kṛṣṇa. Since *sādhana-bhakti* is the process to do this, it is both a paradox and obstacle to put a threshold on how far we are presently willing to go in that relationship.

I would like to bring your attention to how I see this problem manifest for many devotees in their *japa*.

Teaching *Japa* workshops over the years made it apparent to me that many devotees were not chanting well because they were reluctant to fully give themselves to the holy name. I sensed that the reason was that they were afraid that if they surrendered more to the name, the name would cause them to surrender more to Kṛṣṇa and on an unconscious level they didn't want this to happen.

We discussed this point in the workshops and discovered that many devotees didn't want to surrender more than they were comfortable with (for reasons mentioned above, or for any number of other reasons). On some level they feared that good *japa* would push them over their surrender threshold, thus causing them to come to a level of surrender they fear they cannot handle.

In *Śaraṇāgati*, Bhaktivinoda Ṭhākura tells us of his experience with the holy names. He writes that the holy name speaks to Him. What is the holy name saying? What is the message the holy name delivers? What is the holy name ready to tell us if we really listen? The holy name is saying, "Just surrender to Me." But He is doing a lot more than just instructing us to surrender. If we allow Him, the holy name will cause us to give up material attachments, and push us to give our lives fully to Kṛṣṇa.

Why don't we fully experience this? Because we don't want to, because we are afraid to, because on some level we think we'll suffer if we fully surrender.

Fear is a belief in our inability to handle something. Our fear of surrendering is a belief that increased surrender would make life difficult to handle (i.e. we would suffer). So we protect ourselves from allowing the holy name to do this by subtly monitoring our chanting so that we don't fully surrender to the holy name in the mood of, "Kṛṣṇa, do with me whatever you want, whatever is best for our relationship." In other words, we often take baby steps in our surrender to the holy name. (I think I can handle x amount of surrender, so I will only chant with x amount of surrender).

Of course, the reality is that any suffering we experience is a result of our unwillingness to surrender to Kṛṣṇa. Thus, all suffering we experience is self-inflicted, not God-inflicted. This means the only person who is ever going to make us unhappy is ourselves, not Kṛṣṇa. If we have problems surrendering more, it's likely we have gotten this equation backwards.

We discuss this point in our *Japa* workshops to help devotees realize any inhibitions they have about chanting in the mood of full surrender. As devotees become aware of the fears they have about surrender, I ask them to look more closely at these fears. As they do this they begin to see that these fears are not real but are simply their own creations.

At this point, we conduct a *japa* session that focuses on chanting in a more surrendered mood. While chanting, devotees confront their fears of surrender in an attempt to let them go and give themselves more to the holy names. Again, these fears are based on the concern that if I surrender, Kṛṣṇa may do something to make my life more miserable. After the session, they share the experiences and realizations they had while chanting.

One devotee shared a wonderful realization that sums up this article in a better way than I ever could. While chanting she was looking at a picture of Kṛṣṇa she had on her notebook. It was a picture of Kṛṣṇa sitting on a rock by the Yamunā River playing His flute. As she continued to chant, looking at the picture and facing her fears of surrender, the following thought came to her. "How could this beautiful young boy ever do anything to hurt me?"

Tomorrow when you chant your rounds, allow yourself to give up any inhibitions you might have about surrender with this one simple thought.

"How could this beautiful young boy ever do anything to hurt me?"

Note

Surrender doesn't mean acting blindly or without intelligence. Surrender means acting in a way that brings you closer to Kṛṣṇa. This may sometimes mean recognizing a certain nature or tendency that you have and employing it in Kṛṣṇa's service. It can also mean taking extra care of your spiritual practice or health, changing your *āśrama* or service, etc. In rare cases, it can even mean not following an order given to you when you are certain (or have a strong feeling) the results will be spiritually detrimental.

In other words, sometimes surrender can externally look like a selfish act, as if you are compromising or giving into a material tendency. But surrender always means doing what is most favorable for advancing in Kṛṣṇa consciousness.

Act in a way that brings you closer to Kṛṣṇa and helps you think of Kṛṣṇa more. This is surrender. And when you do this, automatically you will be able to help others surrender.

Exercise

Explore your own fears of surrender by finishing this statement. If I fully surrender to Kṛṣṇa , what if _____________?

List as many "what ifs" as you can discover.

Imagine your list was presented to you as if it were a friend's list who wanted your advice in dealing with these exact fears of surrender.

Write down what you would tell him or her for each one of your "what ifs."

Acknowledge that these fears are your creations.

Practice chanting *japa* free of these fears or surrender these fears as you chant.

This exercise is meant to help you realize the illusory nature of your concerns/fears about surrender, that most, if not all of these concerns are your own creations and have no basis in reality. This will enable you to see surrender as something sweet, as something to look forward to, as something easy and natural – and most importantly as something desirable.

By doing this you should see improved results in your chanting. As stated before, these fears inhibit your willingness to call out fully to the name, to let the name control you and take you wherever it desires.

Here are two quotes from Śrīla Prabhupāda to help you surrender. I have bolded several lines that I feel are important to emphasize.

"*Namaḥ* means surrender. *Namaḥ om namaḥ*, this is the way of chanting Vedic mantra. *Om* means addressing the Absolute, and *namaḥ* means "I am surrendering." "Every Vedic mantra is begun *om namaḥ*. *Om* means addressing. **So this mantra is chanted with surrender,** *namaḥ*. **Nothing can be done without**

surrender because our, this conditional life is rebellious life. We have rebelled against the supremacy of the Personality of Godhead... So without surrender, there is no question of making any spiritual progress. Just like a person who has rebelled against the government– the first condition is to surrender; otherwise there is no question of mercy from the government. Similarly anyone, the living entity, anyone of us who has rebelled against the supremacy of the Lord, the beginning of spiritual life is surrender." (*Initiation Lecture, Los Angeles, December 1, 1968*)

"There is no need of material qualifications for making progress on the path of spiritual perfection. In the material world, when one accepts some particular type of service, he is required to possess some particular type of qualification also. Without that, one is unfit for such service. **But in the devotional service of the Lord the only qualification required is surrender. Surrendering oneself is in one's own hand. If one likes, he can surrender unconditionally, without delay, and that begins his spiritual life.**" (*Śrīmad-Bhāgavatam* 2.7.46, Purport)

CHAPTER 3

What Is Guru (Part One)

What is a guru, and who is a disciple?

The śāstras make it clear that taking shelter of a spiritual master is fundamental to the process of Kṛṣṇa consciousness. But what is a guru, and what does it mean to take shelter of a guru? While these questions seem simple, there are nuances that some may not be aware of, and particulars that relate to the unique circumstances of the guru-disciple relationship within ISKCON.

I could write much on this important topic. This is a summary. Due to the depth of the topic, I am dividing this topic into three parts.

I hope this will be of benefit to those looking for a dīkṣā or śīkṣā guru, those who have a guru, and those who are, or may be taking, the role of guru (either dīkṣā or śīkṣā in the future).

We All Should Become Guru

Śrīlā Prabhupāda wanted all his disciples to become gurus. Since everyone who comes to ISKCON is a *śīkṣā* disciple of Srīla Prabhupāda, this means he is asking every one of us to be a guru. Most devotees feel unqualified to be a guru, and thus have difficulty understanding this instruction.

Whenever you help another person, especially one who may be junior to you in Kṛṣṇa consciousness, you are acting as a guru. Guru means one who first shows the path of *bhakti*, one who instructs about *bhakti* and/or one who initiates one into *bhakti*. If you know more than someone else does, you can help them take the next step in Kṛṣṇa consciousness. In the broader sense, you are their teacher, or guru.

Śrīla Prabhupāda's Position

Before discussing the differences and similarities between the *dīkṣā* and *śīkṣā* guru, it is essential to understand that Śrīlā Prabhupāda is everyone's foundational *śīkṣā* guru. Those who begin practicing Kṛṣṇa consciousness connect with Śrīlā Prabhupāda as their *śīkṣā* guru before they think about taking a *dīkṣā* guru.

Anyone can have as intimate a relationship with Śrīlā Prabhupāda as his initiated disciples, since he is personally available to everyone through his books, recordings, and service. This relationship does not replace the need for a *dīkṣā* guru or override the benefit that one can get from a living *śīkṣā* guru. It simply underscores the reality that we are all connected to Śrīlā

Prabhupāda. We are all guided by him and serve him (by serving in ISKCON). All gurus represent him. It is the service of gurus in ISKCON to help disciples come closer to Śrīlā Prabhupāda. In this regard, the Governing Body Commission (GBC) released the following statement in March of 2013:

"Śrīlā Prabhupāda, as the Founder-Ācārya of the International Society for Kṛṣṇa consciousness, is the preeminent guru for all members of ISKCON. All members of ISKCON, for all generations, are encouraged to seek shelter from Śrīlā Prabhupāda. All members of ISKCON are entitled, and encouraged, to have a personal relationship with Śrīlā Prabhupāda through his books, teachings, service, and his ISKCON society."

There Are Many Gurus

In traditional Indian society, the mother is accepted as the first guru. Thus, the child is taught to touch the mother's feet when they first see her in the morning. Even when Brahmānanda Prabhu's mother came to see Śrīlā Prabhupāda, he was instructed by Prabhupāda to touch his mother's feet.

In India, when one subject is studied for many years it is not uncommon for the students to refer to their teacher as their guru. You even find *āśramas* where "disciples" live with their guru to study subjects like music, drama, dance, wrestling, astrology, or Sanskrit.

Honor Is Given to the Guru

Although the details of etiquette may differ from relationship to relationship, the fundamentals of the guru-disciple relationship in the material sphere are similar to the guru-disciple relationship in Kṛṣṇa consciousness. The guru teaches and disciplines the student, and the student honors, respects, and follows their guru as a representative of God.

There Are Many Representatives of God

In the *Śrīmad-Bhāgavatam* (11.17.27), Śrī Kṛṣṇa says "*ācāryaṁ māṁ vijānīyān*" (One should know the *ācārya* (teacher) as Myself). This *śloka* is normally applied to one's *dīkṣā* guru, but when studied within the context of Vedic culture we find that many different persons represent God to their dependents.

The King is accepted as *naradeva*, God's representative. *Śāstra* says that even a guest represents God and should be honored as one would honor God. And as mentioned, the mother, father, and teacher represent God. The Rāmāyaṇa even teaches that 'the husband is the guru for the wife' – *strīṇāṁ bhartā hi daivatam*.

We thus see that honoring another as a representative of God is not exclusive to an official guru-disciple relationship within a spiritual disciplic line. For this reason, the *Bhāgavatam* states that one should not take any superior role unless one is able to deliver his dependents from the cycle of birth and death. In other words, if one takes a superior role, he is responsible to be a guru for his dependents.

Some may think that the formalities of the guru-disciple relationship in Kṛṣṇa consciousness are unique. This thought usually is a result of being raised in a society that does not demonstrate traditional Vedic dynamics of such high regard for superiors.

Who Can Be a Guru?

In ISKCON, there has been – and still may be for some devotees – a misunderstanding of who is qualified to be a guru and what their position is. As mentioned earlier, in the broadest sense of the term, anyone helping you in Kṛṣṇa consciousness is your guru. For example, while a person is giving class, that person is your guru (teacher), and should therefore be respected as such. Of course, after class, such a person may take on a different role in relationship to you, but while giving class you honor them as representing Vyāsadeva.

In the early days, Prabhupāda stated, "By 1975 I want all of my disciples to become gurus." What did Śrīlā Prabhupāda mean? His disciples were all young devotees, not highly elevated or mature in Kṛṣṇa consciousness, so it seemed they were not ready to become *dīkṣā* gurus so soon. One thing is certain: Prabhupāda often spoke of his demise and how he was depending on his disciples to carry on the Kṛṣṇa consciousness movement. Fundamental to this task was the instructing and initiating of disciples. One might logically think that he should have asked his godbrothers to fulfill that role, since it appears that his disciples did not have the qualifications of a guru that we find in *śāstra*, whereas many of his godbrothers were highly advanced and had been initiating disciples for decades.

Prabhupāda did not ask his godbrothers to become gurus in ISKCON; he asked his disciples. Also, Prabhupāda did not say, "I want you to become guru, but it will take you many, many years before you become qualified and perhaps you will never become qualified."

One might question why he didn't say this, because *śāstra* defines a spiritual master as an unalloyed pure devotee; an *uttama bhakta* (topmost devotee), one who is cent per cent engaged in Kṛṣṇa consciousness, has no propensity to criticize others, is always thinking how to save the fallen souls, and never falls down. So naturally the question arises as to what Prabhupāda meant when he told his young disciples that he wanted all of them to become gurus soon. And such a question can be even more confusing in light of the fact that many of the original gurus were unable to strictly maintain their Kṛṣṇa consciousness, although they were some of the most advanced devotees in the movement at the time of Prabhupāda's departure.

Is Guru Synonymous With "Pure Devotee?"

To answer this question, we must first understand how *śāstra*, and Śrīla Prabhupāda, define the term "pure devotee." Prabhupāda once said, "Devotee is a big word. We are trying to be devotees." So, if we are trying to be devotees, and the qualification of a guru is to be a pure devotee, then a guru is rare, especially in ISKCON. It would thus seem that in 1977, few, if any, were qualified to be a guru. But by "pure devotee" Prabhupāda meant something different.

Once Prabhupāda was asked how many pure devotees there are on the planet. He answered with a question: "How many devotees are there in ISKCON?" He was told there are about one thousand devotees in ISKCON. Then he said, "This is how many pure devotees are there on the planet!"

According to *śāstra*, the stage of *madhyama-adhikārī* (the middle stage of *bhakti*) is the beginning stage of pure devotional service. *Madhyama* begins from the stage of *niṣṭhā*, steadiness in *bhakti*. Steadiness in *bhakti* comes after unwanted material desires and tendencies are sufficiently neutralized (*anārtha-nivṛitti*). In this stage, a devotee's *bhakti* is motivated by the desire to please guru and Kṛṣṇa and not by *jñāna* (the desire to be liberated, or to be free from suffering), or by *karma* (the desire for material gain).

The *Nectar of Devotion* defines pure devotional service as service free from *jñāna*, *karma*, etc. This freedom takes place on the *madhyama* platform. Thus, a *madhyama-adhikārī* is a pure devotee. (Thus, in a broader sense, *madhyama* is the beginning stage of *uttama bhakti*).

As a side point, *kaniṣṭha* devotees (the beginning stages of *bhakti*) may act as *madhyamas*, but so long as they are *kaniṣṭha*, they are not permanently situated on the *madhyama* platform. In other words, there is a difference between acting on the *madhyama* platform and being on the *madhyama* platform, just as there is a difference between experiencing *bhāva* (emotion), and steadily being on the platform of *bhāva* (the preliminary stage of love of God).

One who is fixed on the *madhyama* stage is a pure devotee and is engaged in pure devotional service (service not motivated by *jñāna*, *karma* or other desires). Therefore, such a pure devotee can accept disciples. And Prabhupāda encourages such devotees to accept disciples, if not *dīkṣā* disciples, then *śīkṣā* disciples.

Are Dīkṣā Gurus Special?

It is a mistake to believe that because someone is a *dīkṣā* guru in ISKCON, he is necessarily on a higher platform of *bhakti* than others. This misconception often stems from misunderstanding the definition of a pure devotee (as mentioned above), or thinking that because someone gives *dīkṣā*, they must be special or have some special empowerment that others do not have.

In ISKCON, there is a standard set of procedures and requirements for one to become a *dīkṣā* guru, such as one is a loyal follower of Śrīlā Prabhupāda and ISKCON, has good *sādhana*, is qualified to properly guide others in Kṛṣṇa Consciousness, and is visibly on the *madhyama-adhikārī* platform. All those who seek a leadership role in ISKCON are subject to similar requirements. So a devotee does not become different, more special, or elevated overnight to a super status of bhakti by some divine *dīkṣā* guru potency when they become a *dīkṣā* guru. In other words, becoming a *dīkṣā* guru within ISKCON is a service that some devotees feel inspired to take up. As such, there are devotees who are highly advanced in Kṛṣṇa consciousness - sometimes more advanced than some *dīkṣā* gurus - who do not feel they can best serve Śrīlā Prabhupāda by accepting *dīkṣā* disciples.

Many of you reading this, believe it or not, may someday be either asked, or inspired, to take up the service of being a *dīkṣā* guru in ISKCON. Long before you may officially take up this service, you will likely have opportunities to act as a guru to juniors.

In 2013, I received a letter from the GBC secretary informing me that I may now give initiation. Did I immediately have a special guru *śakti* descend on me? Have I become more special, unique, or qualified than those who are not initiating? Did my level of Kṛṣṇa consciousness get automatically upgraded?

It would be nice to get an upgrade as a side benefit of taking up this service. Side benefits (mercy) are, of course, there for all of us when we please Śrīlā Prabhupāda, and if we can please Śrīlā Prabhupāda through this service, then we will get his mercy. And by this mercy we will further advance. And, if we surrender to this service (as with any service) we will get the empowerment to do it. Other than this, there is no unique spiritual power that only those who become *dīkṣā* gurus receive.

What Is a Śikṣā Guru?

To better understand the *dīkṣā* guru and his role in ISKCON, we need to understand the position and role of the *śikṣā* guru as well. One thing I find of essential importance for the preservation and advancement of ISKCON is for devotees to recognize the importance of having a *śikṣā* guru(s) in their lives. There are several reasons why the position of the *śikṣā* guru is important to understand, some philosophical and some practical. So let's look at the position of the *śikṣā* guru in general, and his position in ISKCON, in particular.

Śrīlā Prabhupāda often said that the guru is one. He meant the guru is Kṛṣṇa and all gurus represent Kṛṣṇa by both delivering Kṛṣṇa's message and accepting service on behalf of Kṛṣṇa. As mentioned above, in ISKCON there is a tendency among many to view the *dīkṣā* guru as a special category of guru, and a special category of devotee. This can result in devotees looking only for a *dīkṣā* guru, not understanding there are many *śikṣā* gurus available who can guide them and give them the kind of shelter a *dīkṣā* guru gives. This applies both to those who are initiated and those who are not.

Even for those who have not chosen a *dīkṣā* guru, it is valuable, and in some cases essential, to receive guidance from a *śikṣā* guru, even if they are not planning to take *dīkṣā* in the near future (or even in this lifetime).

When the *Nectar of Devotion* talks about accepting a guru, it explains five ways in which one accepts a guru. Only one of those five relate to formal initiation. This means that the other four also apply to a *śikṣā* guru/disciple relationship whether or not one has a *dīkṣā* guru.

"He mentions the basic principles as follows: (1) accepting the shelter of the lotus feet of a bona fide spiritual master, (2) becoming initiated by the spiritual master and learning how to discharge devotional service from him, (3) obeying the orders of the spiritual master with faith and devotion, (4) following in the footsteps of great *ācārya* (teachers) under the direction of the spiritual master, (5) inquiring from the spiritual master how to advance in Kṛṣṇa consciousness." (*Nectar of Devotion*, Chapter 6)

In Part Two (the next chapter), we will discuss some unhealthy guru/disciple dynamics I have observed over the years in ISKCON.

I Don't Feel Ready to Take Dīkṣā

This following section pertains to those who are not initiated and are not yet aspiring for a *dīkṣā* guru (don't feel ready to take *dīkṣā*).

Because it is helpful for those who are not ready for *dīkṣā* to be guided by a *śikṣā* guru, I wanted to address the reasons one who is not initiated may not choose a guru to take shelter of.

1. One feels unqualified to take *dīkṣā* at the present time.
2. One feels that one will never be ready to chant 16 rounds or follow the four regulative principles in this life.
3. One has not found anyone that they can see as their *dīkṣā* guru.
4. One sees Prabhupāda as their guru and feels that accepting another guru would interfere with that relationship.
5. One is not certain that anyone in ISKCON is qualified to be their guru.
6. One's *dīkṣā* guru fell down and one cannot put faith in another guru.
7. One doesn't feel that they can be a good disciple.

There may be other reasons for not taking shelter of a *śikṣā* guru. Although these concerns are more common when looking for a *dīkṣā* guru, they have less relevance when taking shelter of a *śikṣā* guru.

Taking Shelter of a Śikṣā Guru

Let's go over the above list of reasons that might cause one to not look for a guru, and discuss these reasons in relation to the *śikṣā* guru.

1. *One feels unqualified to take dīkṣā at the present time.*

Not being qualified presently for *dīkṣā* has no bearing on taking shelter of, and getting regular and intimate guidance from, a senior Vaiṣṇava or from having a deep spiritual relationship with this person. Plus, doing so increases one's chances of becoming more quickly qualified for *dīkṣā*.

2. *One feels that one will never be ready to chant 16 rounds and follow the four regulative principles in this life.*

Feeling one may not be qualified for *dīkṣā* in this life should have no bearing on taking shelter of, and getting regular and intimate guidance from a senior Vaiṣṇava and having a deep spiritual relationship with him/her. Plus, the chances of someday becoming qualified for *dīkṣā* will be greater if one takes shelter of a *śikṣā* guru.

3. *One has not found anyone that they can see as their guru.*

One doesn't have to see the *śikṣā* guru within a strict formal guru/disciple context. The *śikṣā* relationship can be more informal and friendly, perhaps more on the lines of a coach, counselor, or mentor. Since faith cannot be artificially imposed, if the instructions given by the *śikṣā* guru are helping the devotee, faith will likely naturally evolve. If this happens, it is a strong guru/disciple relationship that will be the consequence. If the relationship doesn't evolve to this point, it is not a problem. One is still getting the valuable guidance needed to advance.

4. ***One sees Prabhupāda as their guru and feels that accepting another guru would interfere with that relationship.***

One should ask one's *śikṣā* guru to help one deepen one's relationship with Prabhupāda, and act as an intermediary between oneself and Śrīlā Prabhupāda.

5. ***One is not certain that anyone in ISKCON is qualified to be their guru (or even qualified to be anyone's guru).***

To take guidance from a senior Vaiṣṇava, it is not necessary to approach them as a faithful and surrendered disciple. Learn from them and take guidance from them, and see if this helps (you don't have to blindly accept). In this way, the relationship may naturally develop more intimately. If not, still take advantage of the wise guidance you get from them, and show gratitude for this by reciprocating in whatever ways possible.

6. *One's dīkṣā guru fell down and one cannot put faith in another guru.*

Śāstra advises one to take shelter of a guru if one's own guru falls down (it doesn't specifically say to take re-initiation). Of course, many find it most natural to take shelter of Śrīlā Prabhupāda if their guru falls. Yet, for some there remains a vacuum because of a need for a living personal connection. Of course, faith cannot be forced, but connecting with a higher Vaiṣṇava and getting their guidance is always beneficial.

7. *One doesn't feel that they can be a good disciple.*

Generally, no vows are made to the *śikṣā* guru; so being able to chant 16 rounds or follow the four regulative principles doesn't have to be a requirement for being a *śikṣā* disciple. The real requirement is to be sincere about advancing in Kṛṣṇa consciousness. Whatever disqualification one feels they have, it is likely that they will improve more rapidly under the regular guidance of an advanced devotee.

Since getting the association of advanced Vaiṣṇavas is one of the most essential principles of Kṛṣṇa consciousness, both in the stage of *sādhana*, and on the liberated platform, we should cultivate this kind of association and develop close relationships with senior devotees, even before we may feel ready to be a worthy disciple.

Rūpa Gosvāmī advises that we "take shelter of a guru," but he doesn't mean that one cannot take shelter unless one is thinking of taking *dīkṣā* from that person. In fact, devotees sometimes have a more intimate relationship with their *śikṣā* guru than they do with their *dīkṣā* guru.

CHAPTER 4

What Is Guru

(Part Two)

In this chapter, we discuss some flawed understandings of guru-tattva and dive deeper into the understanding of guru-tattva.

Śrīlā Prabhupāda on Guru

I wish to begin by looking at the qualification of the *śīkṣā* and *dīkṣā* gurus in ISKCON. There may be a tendency to magnify the qualities of one's guru in an attempt to reconcile in one's mind the exalted nature of the guru described in *śāstra* with the position of one's own guru, thinking that if he is a guru, he must be on the topmost level of Kṛṣṇa consciousness.

Of course, he may be on that level, but Prabhupāda has indicated many times that seeing Kṛṣṇa face-to-face; being in *līla* with Kṛṣṇa; having descended from the spiritual world; being in direct contact with the Supersoul; and knowing perfectly the past, present and future are not necessary qualifications of a guru. The *madhyama bhakta* can also be a guru if he faithfully explains and follows the teachings of his spiritual master and the previous *ācāryas*.

Prabhupāda said that one who is a good follower becomes a good leader. One who repeats the message as one has heard it, without adding or subtracting anything, who strictly follows the practices of Kṛṣṇa consciousness and dedicates one's life to spreading and teaching Kṛṣṇa consciousness is qualified to take disciples and is a "pure devotee."

It is crucial to understand these qualifications so that we do not:

1. Misunderstand the status of gurus in ISKCON;
2. Create factions of "my guru is the real guru;"
3. Minimize Prabhupāda's instructions to us to become gurus (either *dīkṣā* or *śīkṣā*);

4. Deny that becoming a guru is a service that is accessible to all sincere and strict devotees.

Therefore, all of us – although we may feel we are useless and without any good qualities – can become empowered to guide and save conditioned souls if we sincerely take up the order to be a guru.

Whether we take "guru" to mean a *śīkṣā* or *dīkṣā* guru is not relevant to this discussion. Certainly, I do not mean to minimize the special position of the *dīkṣā* guru, but I do want to emphasize that the qualifications for both are similar.

As another point of clarification, when I use the term *śīkṣā* guru here, I use it in the context of a guru-disciple relationship, not in the sense of a relationship in which one sometimes gets advice from another devotee, or occasionally takes inspiration from their lectures or writings. In other words, I use it here when there is a relationship in which one is regularly guided in one's Kṛṣṇa consciousness and is committed to following and serving their *śīkṣā* guru (although the term *śīkṣā* guru can certainly be used in less formal relationships).

Please Note: In this chapter, I have referred to the *dīkṣā* guru as "he." In 2020, the GBC ratified a resolution acknowledging that women can initiate. Therefore, please note that, while I may make use of the word "he", I am referring to both male and female devotees, i.e., he and/or she.

Some Flawed Understandings of Guru-Tattva:

Due to improper or incomplete understandings of *guru-tattva*, unhealthy practices regarding guru/disciple relations sometimes take place. I shall hereby list some examples.

Scenario 1: You Do Not Recognize Your Guru

A non-initiated devotee is getting regular guidance from one who acts as a *śīkṣā* guru, and the relationship develops nicely. Then, the *śīkṣā* disciple decides to aspire for initiation from another guru, not because there is any problem with the *śīkṣā* relationship, but because the disciple doesn't fully understand that their *śīkṣā* guru could be (or should be) their *dīkṣā* guru. The disciple may not understand this if they are under the impression that a guru is only someone who:

- Is already currently initiating,
- Has many disciples,
- Is a *sannyāsī*,
- Holds important positions in ISKCON or,
- Is special or serves a different purpose to that of a *śīkṣā* guru.

This misunderstanding is not uncommon, and it shows that sometimes a devotee, for reasons mentioned above (or other reasons) may not be able to recognize who their guru really is.

In the above scenario, what can happen is that a devotee's attention begins to be more focused on their *dīkṣā* guru, taking less advantage of the guidance given by the *śīkṣā* guru, which could alter the relationship in other ways. This does not always mean that the devotee will end up being worse off, but sometimes this is the case. In other words, when choosing a *dīkṣā* guru, one should not make the mistake of lessening one's connection with one's *śīkṣā* guru or feel the need to replace one's *śīkṣā* guru with a "real" guru. Of course, some *śīkṣā* gurus do not, or do not want to initiate, but still the relationship with one's *śīkṣā* guru can be as valuable, or even more so, than one's relationship with one's *dīkṣā* guru.

Scenario 2: You Are Uncomfortable Changing Gurus

One may be aspiring for initiation from a well-known guru in ISKCON and then one meets another devotee who gives them the kind of time and guidance that is not possible for that *dīkṣā* guru to give. As such, a very close guru-disciple relationship develops in a manner that the devotee feels is extremely valuable. In some cases, this relationship becomes deeper and more beneficial than the relationship one has with the *dīkṣā* guru they are aspiring for, and taking *dīkṣā* from their *śīkṣā* guru (if the *śikṣa* guru is willing to give it) would be the natural step forward. But, again, the disciple may not recognize this person as a potential *dīkṣā* guru or know that it is okay to accept him as a *dīkṣā* guru and then maintain a *śīkṣā* relationship with the guru from whom the devotee was formerly aspiring to take initiation.

Let us look at some reasons one may feel uncomfortable changing one's choice of *dīkṣā* guru.

- Everyone in one area takes *dīkṣā* from a select group of gurus. Since one has seen these devotees as gurus from the early days of their devotional service, they feel it would be improper, disrespectful, socially unacceptable, or even offensive to not take initiation from one of them (especially if everyone else is doing this).

- The devotees in the area where the aspiring disciple lives are predominately disciples of one or two gurus, so one may feel that they wouldn't get as much support (or be a part of the "family") if one takes *dīkṣā* from someone who has few or no disciples in that area.
- One has had good or long-standing relationships with the prominent *dīkṣā* gurus in one's area, albeit with little personal association between the two.
- One feels it would be offensive to tell the guru one once aspired to take *dīkṣā* from, that they have had a change of heart and wishes to take *dīkṣā* from someone else. It is not actually offensive and is not uncommon. If this does happen, the devotee should ask permission from the guru they once aspired for, to aspire for *dīkṣā* from another devotee. One will then receive blessings to pursue a new relationship.

And there can be other reasons. Of course, one may take *dīkṣā* from the prominent local guru, the one initially aspired for, and still have an intimate relationship with one's *śīkṣā* guru, perhaps even more intimate than with one's *dīkṣā* guru. I certainly don't want to imply that there is anything wrong in choosing a prominent guru, but such decisions should be made in full knowledge of *guru-tattva*, both in terms of philosophy and how the institution of a guru is meant to harmoniously function within ISKCON. In other words, one should not choose a guru simply because everyone else is choosing him.

Scenario 3: You Only Want to Hear From Your Guru

One problem is that devotees only want to hear from their guru. Of course, one should want to hear from their guru. But it is not healthy or pleasing to one's guru if his disciples only attend his programs when he is in town but are rarely seen at other temple programs or functions when he is not present. This is certainly not the way Śrīlā Prabhupāda wanted ISKCON to function.

The Essence of Guru

In the *Nectar of Devotion* (1.1.74), Rūpa Gosvāmī says "*ādau gurv-āśrayaḥ*," in the beginning of spiritual life one should take shelter of a guru. The main aspect of taking shelter is inquiring from the guru and following his instructions. The main function of the guru is not in giving initiation; it is in giving guidance. Of course, initiation is important, but as I said in Part One, one should take shelter of a guru and work under his guidance even if one feels they are not yet ready for formal initiation.

It is primarily through the instructions of the guru, meaning through the execution of these instructions that we advance. Therefore, it is important to note that in our disciplic succession, many of the guru-disciple relationships listed in the *paramparā* are *śīkṣā* relationships, not *dīkṣā* relationships.

The Prominent Role of the Śīkṣā Guru

There are several other common situations in ISKCON, different in nature from what we described above but similar in practice, in which a *śīkṣā* guru plays a significant role in a devotee's life, or could play a significant role if the devotee pursued such a relationship. For example,

- The *dīkṣā* guru gives up strictly following Kṛṣṇa consciousness;
- The *dīkṣā* guru leaves ISKCON;
- The *dīkṣā* guru leaves his body;
- The disciple is doing extended study under someone other than their *dīkṣā* guru;
- The disciple is working closely with another senior devotee, especially someone who is a guru;
- The *dīkṣā* guru and disciple have little contact or interaction (for geographical or other reasons) and the disciple needs regular guidance from a senior devotee.

Śīkṣā and Dīkṣā Are Equal

The prominence of either a *dīkṣā* or *śīkṣā* guru in the life of a devotee will vary according to individual circumstances, and sometimes a *śīkṣā* guru-disciple relationship develops so naturally that to minimize the relationship would be both unfortunate and disrespectful.

If one sees and treats the person they take guidance from like a guru, it is good (and proper) to acknowledge that an ongoing *śīkṣā* relationship exists (or is wanted), that one values it, and that one wants to maintain it.

CHAPTER 5

What Is Guru
(Part Three)

In this chapter, I conclude our discussion on guru-tattva by approaching this topic from the perspective of a guru. I humbly believe that, in doing so, I speak on behalf of other gurus, both dīkṣā and śīkṣā (including counselors, mentors, and teachers) and thus present their vision and realizations as well.

The Guru's Perspective

I guide many devotees who are not ready for initiation, or not even thinking about initiation. Through the exchanges we have I can see how their willingness to be guided, to reveal their problems, to "take shelter," and to apply what I suggest helps them in many ways. I can see how this guidance will enable many of them to someday become qualified to take initiation.

Does this mean they should someday become my initiated disciples? This is a good question.

First, let us understand that I do not have to be (or may not be) the only person from whom they receive regular instructions, or with whom they have a close relationship. Since one can have many *śīkṣā* gurus, it is common that one may find guidance and inspiration in many places. One should never feel this is wrong, and thus limit the wonderful guidance they can get from the many senior devotees in ISKCON. If we see the oneness of guru, that Kṛṣṇa is the guru, and that the guru represents Kṛṣṇa and Prabhupāda, then we see the oneness of all gurus in their guidance and desire to help us advance in Kṛṣṇa consciousness. In this sense, we should be open to taking guidance from many, and to take more shelter of any devotee that inspires us, even if he is not a *dīkṣā* guru and does not plan to become a *dīkṣā* guru.

So, should those who take shelter of a *śīkṣā* guru eventually take initiation from him? There is no right or wrong answer. Taking initiation from a guru is a matter of personal choice. For example, let us say a guru is giving guidance to someone and they are advancing well, but simultaneously they have been getting guidance or inspiration from several other devotees, including some *dīkṣā* gurus. After years of predominantly taking guidance from one guru, would it be wrong for them to one day tell him that they have been accepted by so and so to become his disciple and will be initiated in six months?

As I mentioned before, this is normal and common. The case where it may be somewhat abnormal is:

1. When the *śīkṣā* relationship is stronger;
2. When the *śīkṣā* relationship is more beneficial than the relationship one has with the *dīkṣā* guru (and the *śīkṣā* guru is also a *dīkṣā* guru);
3. If the decision was made due to pressure;
4. If the decision was made for any reasons that are not fundamental to the choice of a *dīkṣā* guru (of course, if one's *śīkṣā* guru is not giving *dīkṣā*, such a choice is necessary).

Who Is My Guru?

Take *śīkṣā* from many sources. After doing so for some time, it should become more and more obvious that one of these devotees inspires, helps, guides, relates to, motivates and builds your faith and desire to surrender in a special way. That is normally the person from whom you would ask initiation (provided they give initiation).

For devotees who are making a decision about whom to approach for *dīkṣā*, and for those who help devotees in making these decisions, I would like to offer some helpful points for consideration that are gleaned from real life in ISKCON. I do not offer these points as the absolute criteria for choosing a guru, but as points to consider when deciding on who you eventually may want to take initiation from.

1. *How Often Will You See Your Guru?*

Does he live or travel in parts of the world that are far from where you live and rarely, if ever, come to where you live? In other words, is it important for you to have some regular personal contact with your guru, or are e-mail and online classes sufficient?

2. *Can You Correspond With Him Regularly?*

Is he too busy or does he have too many disciples for you to receive regular personal instructions or instructions via e-mail or social media? This question also should take into account how often you feel you will need personal instructions. Of course, some gurus can provide such instructions through their senior disciples whose association is more easily available; or some devotees will be able to get this kind of guidance from others and be satisfied with this. However, others might feel isolated from (or even neglected by) their guru when it is not possible for him to give regular (or even any) personal guidance.

3. *Can You Help Him in His Service?*

For some devotees it is important to have direct service to their guru. If this is important to you, consider if there will be opportunity and facility for this?

Also, consider if he emphasizes, or works on, projects that do not relate to your service, or service that you are not interested in or inclined to work on. Is his focus, for example, on developing *varṇāśrama* and working on farm projects, whereas your nature and inclination is to develop preaching programs in big cities? Will his emphasis on these specific projects make you feel awkward – even guilty – that you are not working on his projects? Could this even undermine your enthusiasm for the projects you are working on? Does he tend to be more traditional, strict, formal, etc. in his approach to teaching or practicing Kṛṣṇa consciousness or more liberal?

Other aspects of his personality/nature that you may take into consideration are how philosophical, academic, soft, disciplinary, etc. he may be. In other words, do you relate well to his nature and style of preaching Kṛṣṇa consciousness?

4. Do His Actions Represent Your Idea of Guru?

Do you have an image of a guru who is orthodox, thereby making it difficult for you to follow a guru who does not adhere to these standards? Or does he adhere to standards that are, in your mind, too formal, strict, old-fashioned, or orthodox, and thus not relatable to you?

You may think these considerations to be mundane, but Bhaktivinoda Ṭhākura, in quoting Sanātana Gosvāmī's advice that the guru and disciple observe one another for one year, says that part of this process of observation is to determine if the guru and disciple are a good match. It could happen in the future that you have difficulty accepting instructions or opinions from your guru because of some or all the above reasons. These are realities we should be aware of.

Expectations

Connected to the list above is the problem of expectations. A disciple may have certain expectations at the time of choosing a guru or receiving initiation. Expectations that either the guru cannot fulfill, that no guru can or should fulfill, or that circumstances may later make it difficult or impossible for the guru to fulfill. Therefore, it is important for both the guru and disciple to be clear about expectations.

It is important to know that the guru's perceived inability to fulfill some of these expectations is not simply related to his nature or limitations (he won't spend time counseling female disciples, deal with householder problems, etc.). But they may be based on a misunderstanding that you have of a guru's position. Some prospective disciples have, as I explained, a stereotyped (mis) understanding of the position of their guru, and may feel let down in the future when they find out that their guru is not a *mahā-bhāgavata* who is directly speaking to Rādhārāṇī, doesn't have extraordinary powers, doesn't exhibit ecstatic symptoms, may not understand the finer points of rāsa, etc.

One of the original eleven gurus in ISKCON tells us that his early disciples used to glorify him by saying that, "He is taking *prasādam* with Rādhārāṇī." After a number of gurus fell down and ISKCON devotees became clearer about what a guru is and isn't, this kind of glorification changed to, "Thank you, Gurudeva, for steadily following the regulative principles." The understanding is that the main qualifications of a guru are to be an obedient follower of his guru, relating the teachings of his guru perfectly, and is dedicated to giving Kṛṣṇa to others.

The Institution or the Person?

Often, more than making a personal connection with the guru, one makes a connection with the institution of the guru: the many disciples, books, programs, etc., that the guru has. For some devotees, this is exactly what inspires them. This gives them what they want and need. They feel sheltered by the guru's organization as well as programs and projects the guru has developed. Others who want or need a more personal connection would do better to find a guru who can give them more personal guidance.

On the other hand, sometimes a devotee may choose a guru with many disciples to avoid a deep personal connection with him, and in this way become less accountable to his guru. This, of course, is not the basis for choosing a guru.

Looking Back

Some devotees today look back on the time when they accepted their guru, and realize that they made less of a personal choice and more of a social choice, sometimes even accepting the *dīkṣā* guru at the expense of recognizing the deep relationship they had (or potentially could/should have had) with their *śīkṣā* guru. In retrospect, they realize that at the time they were unable to understand or acknowledge that their *śīkṣā* guru was indeed a real guru, someone who played – and could have continued to play – a more significant role in their life if only they had recognized the importance of that relationship.

Or this happens later when they meet another guru and think, "If I had met you earlier, I would have taken *dīkṣā* from you instead."

You might then ask, "Should I necessarily take *dīkṣā* from the *śīkṣā* guru who is giving me the most significant guidance?" Ultimately, every situation is different and personal, and there may be advantages or disadvantages to this. However, Śrīla Prabhupāda does say that generally the *śīkṣā* guru can become one's *dīkṣā* guru.

Concluding Words

What I have done in these chapters is made you aware of important guru/disciple dynamics and given various perspectives on this issue for your personal consideration. It is not a black and white issue. Sometimes, just having an advanced devotee as one's guru, knowing that he is powerfully engaged in devotional service, having access to his lectures, feeling his mercy through following his instructions, being engaged in service, and also having good *saṅga* is all one needs to be perfectly situated in Kṛṣṇa consciousness. For others, they are most inspired if they can personally serve his preaching mission. And for still others, having some personal contact throughout the year is essentially important.

Śrīlā Prabhupāda asked all of his disciples to become gurus and accept their own disciples, whether it be as *śīkṣā* or *dīkṣā*.

Devotees accept the position of guru as a service to him, a service to ISKCON, and a service to their disciples. The success of this service depends on following the instructions of Śrīlā Prabhupāda, passing those instructions on to others, and setting an example by living those instructions. Every bona fide guru does this and is thus capable of bringing their disciples to the lotus feet of Kṛṣṇa. Still, as one of my godbrothers said, "There are different lids for different pots."

Speaking for myself – and I believe I speak for other gurus – whatever good qualities you see in us, whatever success we have, or whatever opulence we possess, are all due to Prabhupāda's mercy. Failing to follow his orders will turn us into ordinary people battling with our mind and senses, trying to squeeze out some happiness from this world. Therefore, any glorification of Prabhupāda's disciples who have become gurus is direct glorification of Śrīlā Prabhupāda, and any service offered to them is service to Prabhupāda. Prabhupāda wanted his disciples to be glorified. He said the more they are glorified, the more he is glorified. And of course, they are glorious because they serve Prabhupāda, the most glorious.

SECTION THREE

Creating Balance in Your Life

CHAPTER 1

Integration – Balancing Opposites

As you may know, I often write about issues related to the mind, emotions, and our conditioned nature, and address problems that are common to many devotees. In this chapter, I deal with one such problem: the opposing forces that exist within us. We have Kṛṣṇa conscious ideals, yet our conditioned nature often wants the opposite, resisting our deepest spiritual desires.

We need to find a middle ground – a place in which we acknowledge these competing natures and integrate them so we become balanced. In this section, I discuss how to do this.

The approach I use is largely psychological. I have purposely chosen this approach in response to requests I receive to deal with issues that affect our spiritual lives from a psychological perspective.

This problem of duality within us is discussed in the Mādhurya-kādambinī by Śrīla Viśvanāth Cakravārtī Ṭhākura. Of course, the solution to all problems is to advance in Kṛṣṇa consciousness, because the problems we face are due to contact with the modes of nature. The approach I take, however, is also important. It will help us deal with our specific conditioning in a way that makes it easier for us to practice Kṛṣṇa consciousness from where we are at today.

Spiritual Schizophrenia

Without integrating our opposing natures, we can live like a "spiritual schizophrenic." For example, we appreciate the value of humility and thus desire to avoid fault-finding and become more aware of our faults. We also make an effort to appreciate and humbly serve the devotees, and avoid attracting attention to ourselves. Yet, we also find within ourselves a strong tendency to find fault, as well as the need for recognition and appreciation. We may even become upset or dejected if we don't get the acknowledgement or praise we believe we deserve. This negative side often causes guilt because our actions are out of alignment with our values.

Don't Deny Your Feelings

How do we deal with this?

The worst thing we can do is deny or suppress the contradictory feelings. Don't run away from or try to bury uncomfortable emotions. Acknowledge the saint and the sinner within, without resistance. The more we connect with the uneasy feelings that accompany material tendencies, the more we will naturally integrate them through the intelligence of our emotions.

What does "intelligence of our emotions" mean? As mentioned above, guilt sends us a message that we are out of alignment. Thus, the process of integration, as I refer to here, is not a mental or intellectual exercise in which we analyze our feelings. It is allowing us to feel – to experience two opposite emotions simultaneously.

In doing so, the integration and balancing of opposite forces begins to happen naturally.

Integration comes when the polar opposites of desiring to be a saint and desiring to be a sinner find a balance. It is balancing the desire to be advanced beyond our realization with the desire to do (or fear of doing) something wrong, sinful, or degrading. The result is that we become a more unified and healthier person, someone who relates to, accepts, and integrates both sides of himself. We function happily and enthusiastically without being overly influenced by the extremes of attraction or repulsion. Otherwise, our attractions and repulsions can push our life around.

I Love You – I Hate You

Let's look at a common example. A man appreciates sexual control and detachment, yet is very attracted to women. It is common that he will either resist acknowledging this attraction or resist experiencing how this makes him feel, which can manifest as false detachment, repulsion, or even infatuation with women.

In this case, integration is the center point between excessive desire to enjoy women and excessive desire to avoid them. When a man integrates in this area, his interactions with women become healthy because there is less attraction and repulsion. He will then make a better *brahmacārī* or *gṛhastha.*

When we are better able to integrate extremes, we will more easily accept where we are at without being overwhelmed by the "sinner within," or frustrated by our inability to acquire immediate fulfillment of our higher spiritual aspirations.

Polar Opposites are Pulling Me

It is important to find integration within our *varṇa* and *āśrama*. Otherwise, we may end up in love/hate relationships with people, spouses, services, or occupations. For example, when not integrated, a married man who confronts constant difficulties in household life may lament that he should have remained single, or he dreams of leaving his family responsibilities prematurely.

An older single man, in confronting his attraction to women, may regret not having married when he was younger, even though it is too late in his life to marry.

How does being out of balance affect work and service? I may love doing something, but then I do it 16 hours a day and either end up hating the very thing I love, or love doing it so much that I neglect other important aspects of my life. Thus, what I love becomes the cause of disturbance.

Let us look at the dualities that relate to *sādhana*. I relish chanting, but I also procrastinate on my rounds. I like the early morning hours for *sādhana*, but I like to stay up late, or I sleep more than I need. I relish *sādhana*, but I'm a workaholic, and thus I ruin my *sādhana* by allowing my work to be all-consuming. I love to read and learn *śāstra*, but I also like to chill out or waste my study time in frivolous activities.

Integration Is the Solution

Everything naturally aligns and flows without intense attraction or repulsion when integrated. If polar opposites are too extreme, then we tend to oscillate between them rather than become a balanced combination of both.

Until we become more advanced, these contradictions will exist within us – at least to some degree. Therefore, we need to face these dualities and deal with them well. Doing so will begin to cure our "spiritual schizophrenia."

Exercise

Think of two opposing desires you have. It can also be a desire for something and a resistance to the very thing you desire. Think of what you desire and allow yourself to experience the feeling this desire produces.

Next, while feeling this desire, think of the exact opposite desire (or your resistance to what you want). Allow yourself to experience both of these polar opposites simultaneously and to their fullest. Feel the energy of these desires within you as opposite poles coming together and beginning to integrate.

Some other examples of this are:

- I want to be a more surrendered soul, but I cherish my "freedom" and "independence."
- I want to be self-disciplined, but I love to be spontaneous, or strongly resist too much discipline.

- I want to live a simpler life, but love to spend, collect, and expand.
- I want to start important Kṛṣṇa conscious projects, but don't want to take responsibility for getting these projects going.
- I have a strong desire to be peaceful, friendly, and kind, but I easily become angry, intolerant, and nasty.
- I want to be more compassionate and thus do something to help others become Kṛṣṇa conscious, but I resist doing the austerity required to do this.
- I want to work together with a group and be a team player, but I like being a loner, controller, or dictator (or all three).

CHAPTER 2

Balancing Dependence and Independence

Śrīla Prabhupāda, śāstra and the ācāryas have spoken about being totally dependent on guru and Kṛṣṇa. Independence, we learn, is our disease. It is what brought us to the material world and what keeps us here. Is there such a thing, however, as too much dependence and not enough independence?

In this section, we explore the balance between dependence and independence.

Equipoised

In the *Bhagavad-gītā*, we find the word for balance, *samaḥ* translated as "equipoised." The dictionary defines the word "equipoised" as a state in which various parts form a satisfying and harmonious whole, and no part is out of proportion or unduly emphasized at the expense of other parts. Arjuna is out of balance. He is the world's finest warrior. He is being asked to protect religion and morality by going to battle. He refuses, choosing a life of renunciation and asceticism out of compassion for the opposing warriors, his kinsmen. Kṛṣṇa speaks to put him back into balance.

"Perform your duty equipoised, O Arjuna, abandoning all attachment to success or failure. Such equanimity is called *yoga*." (*Bhagavad-gītā* 2.48)

The *Gītā* devotes much of its dialogue to help Arjuna create balance in his life.

"One who is equal to friends and enemies, who is equipoised in honor and dishonor, heat and cold, happiness and distress, fame and infamy...is very dear to Me." (*Bhagavad-gītā* 12.18-19)

Even after Arjuna overcame his resistance to the war, he was still hesitant to personally participate in the fight. Even though Kṛṣṇa told Arjuna, "They are already put to death by My arrangement," (*Bhagavad-gītā* 11.33) He still wanted Arjuna to fight. To let Arjuna off the hook would keep him out of balance.

Kṛṣṇa wanted Arjuna to fight with balance and without attachment, to do it because it was the right thing to do. In fact, because Arjuna's compassion and detachment were unsuitable for the situation, Kṛṣṇa spoke the *Gītā* to get Arjuna angry enough to bring the balance back into his *kṣatriya* nature.

When Dependence and Independence Are Out of Balance

Now that we have established that balance is a fundamental theme in the *Gītā*, and thus fundamental to a stable material and spiritual life, let's look at the balance between being dependent on guru and Kṛṣṇa and being independently strong.

Śāstra exalts the position of total dependance. Bhaktivinoda Ṭhākura and other *ācāryas* have written many songs in which they clearly express their complete dependence on the mercy of guru and Kṛṣṇa. In the *Gītā*, independence is described as an *asuric* quality.

"The demoniac person thinks: '...I am the lord of everything. I am the enjoyer. I am perfect, powerful and happy. I am the richest man, surrounded by aristocratic relatives. There is none so powerful and happy as I am. I shall perform sacrifices, I shall give some charity, and thus I shall rejoice.' In this way, such persons are deluded by ignorance." (*Bhagavad-gītā* 16.13-15)

Can this attitude of dependence, however, be misunderstood and thus cause negative results? Can we be so dependent that we can't function well in the absence of our guru or very advanced devotees? Or can we err on the side of independence to compensate for being too dependent, and thus develop what we believe to be a "healthier" attitude when it actually isn't? Both are possible, and both are not uncommon.

Can't Live Without My Guru

I used to live in Los Angeles, and Śrīla Prabhupāda would visit there every year. I distinctly remember the temple population increasing when Prabhupāda came (in the early days he would stay for months at a time), and decreasing shortly after he left. When Prabhupāda came to L.A., devotees we hadn't seen since Prabhupāda's last arrival would show up, enthusiastically participate in devotional service, and then disappear into material life a week or so after Prabhupāda left.

This phenomenon is even more apparent, and understandably so, when the guru leaves his body. Some devotees are unable to maintain their Kṛṣṇa consciousness well – if at all – after the departure of their guru from this world.

I have lived through another phenomenon: the falling down of several gurus I was closely working with. A very telling thing takes place when this happens: some disciples fall apart and become very weak, or they leave Kṛṣṇa consciousness altogether.

Some disciples, on the other hand, become stronger.

The Disciple Always Lives With the Guru

This doesn't mean a disciple should not be attached to his guru or advanced devotees, not want their personal association, not want to personally serve them, or not be dependent on their instructions. The problem lies in becoming so dependent on another's mercy that one's needs for personal association or guidance become unhealthy and disempowering.

Yes, Prabhupāda did acknowledge the value of personal association. We all benefited tremendously from it and would go out of our way to get it. Prabhupāda was generous with his association. When a senior devotee had a problem or became weak, Prabhupāda would often invite the devotee to travel with him for a short time to regain his strength or suggest that he spend time with a fixed-up devotee. Also, Prabhupāda constantly traveled to give disciples his association. Therefore, it's not that Prabhupāda minimized the value of personal association. At the same time, (we're talking about balance) he did say that *vāṇī* (the words of the spiritual master) is more important than *vapuḥ* (personal association), and that the disciple lives with the guru by following his instructions.

I had personal experience of this. When Prabhupāda arrived in San Francisco for the 1970 Ratha-yātrā festival, I, along with a temple room packed with shaven-headed *brahmacārīs*, greeted him. He was so pleased to see us that he stopped at the temple room entrance for a few moments, relishing this wonderful site. He stood gazing over us with a smile that revealed the great pleasure he was feeling in seeing his movement expand. He then entered the temple, sat on his *vyāsāsana*, and began to chant *Śrī Gurvaṣṭakam*, prayers to his spiritual master. I had never seen Prabhupāda chant these prayers on his arrival to any temple, and I am not aware he ever did this again when arriving at a temple.

Why did he do this? It was a bit of a mystery. This mystery was later solved when the temple leaders revealed that Prabhupāda told them how he was so pleased to see such a large number of effulgent devotees that he called for his Guru Mahārāja to come and see.

This reminds us that Prabhupāda said that he never felt alone in his early days in New York. He always felt that he was with his guru.

While on *saṅkīrtana*, those who distribute Prabhupāda's books feel a special closeness with him, a closeness his disciples would sometimes not even feel while sitting at his feet. Of course, all of Prabhupāda's disciples relished sitting at his feet and hearing from him, but when a devotee with important service would forgo the opportunity to be with Prabhupāda to undertake this service, Prabhupāda appreciated it.

Our Co-Pilot

What is healthy dependence and what is unhealthy (dysfunctional) dependence? Prabhupāda used to say that every one of us must fly our own plane. We learn from our guru how to fly (dependence), and then fly our plane via his instructions (independence). As we follow his instructions, we feel even closer to him, as if he is sitting beside us. In other words, he is always our co-pilot.

In addition, flight school training never ends. The guru is continually teaching us how to improve our flying skills.

When Relationships Become Dysfunctional

The word "dysfunctional" is popularly used today with regard to relationships. When a person's happiness, or their ability to function normally, is too dependent on another person, their relationship is considered dysfunctional. How would this apply to Kṛṣṇa consciousness? Prabhupāda said that we should feel like a fool before our spiritual master. This means we should not proudly sit in front of our guru thinking, "I also know many things about life. I even know some things he doesn't know." Rather, we should think, "I am such a fool that I wasted unlimited lives in useless material pursuits and have thus remained entangled in material life since time immemorial. By my so-called knowledge I became expert at causing myself suffering. My guru is the one who can help (and is helping) me get out of this material entanglement. On my own, I could never do it."

After telling us we should feel like a fool before our guru, Prabhupāda said, "But you should not act like a fool." In other words, the instructions are there so we can stop being foolish.

No Strength of My Own

One devotee tells of his battles in his early days of Kṛṣṇa consciousness. When he was opening a new center, his enthusiasm to continue came solely from the regular letters he received from Prabhupāda. Each letter gave him enough energy to continue for another week. If he didn't receive a letter within seven days, he would end up discouraged and depressed, sleeping for most of the day. As soon as he received the next letter, he would again become enlivened for about a week. He found no strength within himself to continue without the constant encouragement and pushing he received in those letters.

No doubt we need encouragement and pushing, but Kṛṣṇa consciousness doesn't mean being so dependent on one's guru or senior association that one cannot function well without constant inspiration, supervision, and guidance. When Śrīla Prabhupāda left us, we all had difficulty. This is to be expected; but devotees who had the most association with Prabhupāda often had the most difficulty living in his absence. His personal presence had become so essential to their spiritual lives that their Kṛṣṇa consciousness could not thrive without it.

Always With My Spiritual Master

During the first years after Prabhupāda's departure, we struggled to realize how he was still present with us. Those that survived did so by realizing that hearing Prabhupāda's instructions and spreading his mission were how to remain most intimately connected with him. This realization still keeps Prabhupāda's disciples alive and well in Kṛṣṇa consciousness today.

It has been my experience that the more responsibility I take up in Śrīla Prabhupāda's mission, the closer I feel to him, and the more I feel with him. The more I try to be the devotee Prabhupāda wanted me to be, the more I feel him guiding me. Association through separation is tangible, but it takes the proper consciousness to realize it.

We Are Already Blessed

The instructions of the guru are meant to make the disciple a pure devotee. A pure devotee imbibes the best of both worlds: being both self-sufficient and totally dependent. The dependence is on the instructions of the guru, while the independence is the strength and willpower to follow those instructions.

Prabhupāda writes:

"Kṛṣṇa consciousness Movement is for training men to be independently thoughtful and competent in all types of departments of knowledge and action...There must be always individual striving and work and responsibility, competitive spirit, not that one shall dominate and distribute benefits to the others and they do nothing but beg from you and you provide. No. Never mind there may be botheration to register each centre, take tax certificate each, become separate corporations in each state. That will train men how to do these things, and they shall develop reliability and responsibility, that is the point." (Letter: December 22, 1972)

The strength to follow the instructions is also the mercy of the guru, but the mercy is something that the disciple activates by his own willingness to inquire, serve, and surrender. One devotee asked Prabhupāda for his mercy so that he would be able to follow his instructions. Prabhupāda replied, "My instructions are my mercy." Devotees often ask for blessings from senior devotees. This is natural, and we need their blessings, but we should always remember that the real blessings are their words and service. The *sādhus* bless us with their instructions; we bless ourselves by following those instructions.

Don't Be a Leaky Tire

Should we get the association of our guru(s) or advanced devotees whenever possible?

Yes.

Should we always want to hear the instructions of our guru(s) and should our lives be dependent on those instructions?

Yes.

The goal, however, is to become a living example of those instructions, to utilize those instructions to grow and to become stronger. In this way, we will attain the perfect balance of healthy dependence and personal initiative, fully utilizing the mercy that comes through following those instructions.

Otherwise, we can become a leaky tire that needs to be blown up constantly.

We need to:

- Intelligently understand both the instructions given to us, as well as how they apply to our lives.
- Know how to adjust two apparently contradictory instructions.
- Know when an instruction may not be applicable in a certain situation.
- Know that our guru lives in his instructions and we live with him by following those instructions.

Too Much Independence

How do we err on the side of being too independent? When disciples of Prabhupāda disobeyed an instruction of his, considering it could be done in a better way, or that it was a compromise of Vaiṣṇava principles, Prabhupāda often called these disciples "over-intelligent." When we use our intelligence in a way that is not aligned with guru, *sādhu* and *śāstra*, we are being over-intelligent. This is certainly a misuse of independence. Reflecting upon my early days in Kṛṣṇa consciousness, I realized that I wasn't "smart" enough to disobey Prabhupāda's instructions. As I became more "intelligent", I found the tendency in myself to "intelligently" disobey.

We also misuse independence when we identify the abilities Kṛṣṇa gives us as our own, and then become overconfident. One devotee relates that after becoming the number one book distributor in his zone, he became overly proud. Kṛṣṇa then decided to humble him. As long as he remained proud, practically everyone he approached refused to take a book. Kṛṣṇa clearly told him, "It's not you who is distributing these books."

We feel good thinking, "I did it." Kṛṣṇa feels good teaching us, "You didn't do it."

Arjuna Achieves Balance

Arjuna finally understood what Kṛṣṇa wanted him to do. He told Kṛṣṇa, "I am now firm and free from doubt and am prepared to act according to Your instructions." (*Bhagavad-gītā* 18.73). It was only when he came to a balanced state that he could do this. He was no longer attached to not fighting or attached to fighting. He was attached to what Kṛṣṇa wanted. When out of balance with his attachments and aversions, he couldn't do what Kṛṣṇa wanted. Once he had attained balance, resuming his role as a *kṣatriya*, fighting valiantly became natural.

Similarly, with a balanced relationship with our guru and advanced devotees, we have the kind of dependence that results in a healthy independence.

Feel like a fool. Just don't act like one.

CHAPTER 3

The Balance Between Effort and Mercy

What is the relationship between effort and mercy? How much of our advancement depends upon our own efforts and how much depends upon the mercy we receive? In other words, can mercy actually be earned, and if so, how? And if it is earned, is it actually mercy?

In this section, I will address all these questions.

Who Is in Control?

How much control do we have over our spiritual advancement? It seems like we have a lot of control. After all, our choices affect our future. Yet Bhaktivinoda Ṭhākura says, "Your mercy is everything to me." This makes it sound like it is only through mercy that we advance. So how much of our progress depends upon the mercy of guru and Kṛṣṇa, and how much depends on our own effort?

Great devotees pray, "Kṛṣṇa, I don't have any qualification to practice bhakti, what to speak about achieving it. I don't even have the desire to practice *bhakti*." Śrīla Bhaktivinoda Ṭhākura says, "My Lord, if you examine me, you will find that I have no good qualities. Therefore, please do not judge my qualifications. If you judge me, I have no hope."

We plead to the judge for his mercy, and if the judge is merciful, he will reduce, or even dismiss, our sentence. Mercy means we are receiving something we don't deserve. We might deserve to be in prison for our entire life, but if the judge shows mercy, he will reduce the sentence – or even let us go free. Mercy carries the connotation that we receive something we don't deserve. We get what we haven't earned.

This mood may cause us to conclude that if we have no qualifications, whatever progress we make will be entirely dependent on the mercy of the Lord. We acknowledge that our past is so sinful that if Kṛṣṇa were to apply justice to our case, we would have no chance of entering the path of *bhakti*. This can make us believe that our own effort is of little or no value, and our progress is totally dependent on Kṛṣṇa's mercy.

This is true. But it's not the whole story.

Śrīla Bhaktisiddhānta perfectly solves this dilemma in the following statement:

"Unless we extend our best efforts earnestly, and qualify ourselves for the Lord's mercy, it is next to impossible that we can be rescued from our fallen condition." (From *Thakura Upadeshu Upakdhyanamarkata-o-marjaranyaya*).

I find the statement "and qualify ourselves for the Lord's mercy" enlightening. Qualify ourselves for mercy seems like a paradox. If I am qualified, it's not mercy; if I am not qualified, it is. What's going on here?

It's true: we could not have taken up the path of *bhakti* in our present condition unless Kṛṣṇa overlooked our disqualifications for practicing *bhakti*. However, there is more to this.

Ye yathā māṁ prapadyante (*Bhagavad-gītā* 4.11), Kṛṣṇa says that He reciprocates with the mood, devotion, attitude, and effort of His devotees. Kṛṣṇa is saying He is responsive. If we give nothing, we get nothing. But if we give a little to Kṛṣṇa, we get back much more than we gave. This is the meaning of mercy.

How Much Mercy Do You Need?

Kṛṣṇa says in the *Gītā* that He gives intelligence to the sincere devotee so he can come back to Kṛṣṇa. How much of this intelligence Kṛṣṇa gives will depend on how much of it we need. If our needs to go back to Godhead are small, we'll get a small amount of intelligence. If our needs are great, we will get a great amount of intelligence. This intelligence is Kṛṣṇa's mercy on us. The amount we get, or don't get, is dictated by our desire. Anyone can get Kṛṣṇa's mercy, but devotees are the ones who show Kṛṣṇa they want it. We don't just sit down and wait for mercy. We pray for it and we act in a way to get it. We make the first move. Kṛṣṇa could have done everything in the battle of Kurukṣetra, but He wanted Arjuna to do it. Once Arjuna stood up to fight, Kṛṣṇa did the rest. This means that it is not bhakti to sit down and expect Kṛṣṇa to do everything for us.

"O Bhārata, stand and fight."

Śrīla Bhaktisiddhānta tells us that we cannot get out of the material entanglement without Kṛṣṇa's mercy, yet we are told that the *mahātmās* constantly endeavor for perfection. Still confused? Is there a formula? Is it 10% effort and 90% mercy? The answer is found in the pastime of Dāmodara.

Two Fingers Short

Once, mother Yaśodā wanted to punish Kṛṣṇa for being naughty. So she decided to tie Him up so He couldn't do more mischief. But the rope she was using was too short. So she went and brought more rope, but strangely it was still too short. She couldn't figure out what the problem was. To make sure the rope would be long enough, she borrowed ropes from the neighbors. Cowherd men have lots of ropes, and she got enough rope to tie Him up many times over. Yet it was still two fingers short. She was trying, trying, and trying to tie Kṛṣṇa up, and He wouldn't allow it. Finally, when she was totally exasperated,

Kṛṣṇa agreed to be bound by her (love). In a commentary on this verse by Viśvanātha Cakravartī Ṭhākura, he says that the two fingers represent effort and mercy. So how much effort is enough? As much effort as Kṛṣṇa decides we need to put forth. As Prabhupāda says, "God is not cheap." We do have to pay a price for mercy. But we pay little and get much.

sarvasya cāhaṁ hṛdi sanniviṣṭo
mattaḥ smṛtir jñānam apohanaṁ ca

"I am seated in everyone's heart, and from Me come remembrance, knowledge and forgetfulness." (*Bhagavad-gītā* 15.15)

Kṛṣṇa gives us what we desire (which works well when we desire Him). However, if we don't desire Him, a word of caution is in place. Be careful what you desire. You might just get it.

Kṛṣṇa Resides in the Heart

According to Christian philosophy, Jesus is knocking at the door of our heart. We open the door and let him in. If you let him in, you will be free from your sinful activities and go back to heaven. But Vaiṣṇavas understand that Kṛṣṇa is already in the heart. So there is no outside door to open. But if He is already in our hearts, then why are we not automatically becoming purified? The story of Kṛṣṇa wanting to hide from Kaṁsa is interesting. Kṛṣṇa says if I hide in his heart, he won't find Me because he won't be able to see Me there. So Kṛṣṇa can hide in our hearts for lifetimes, and since we don't know He is there, or we don't turn to Him, we don't get purified.

In the spiritual world Kṛṣṇa does not exist in our hearts. He only exists in our hearts in the material world. Why? To guide us back to Him – or to guide us away from Him.

īśvaraḥ sarva-bhūtānāṁ
hṛd-deśe 'rjuna tiṣṭhati
bhrāmayan sarva-bhūtāni
yantrārūḍhāni māyayā

"The Supreme Lord is situated in everyone's heart, O Arjuna, and is directing the wanderings of all living entities, who are seated as on a machine, made of the material energy." (*Bhagavad-gītā* 18.61)

sarvasya cāhaṁ hṛdi sanniviṣṭo
mattaḥ smṛtir jñānam apohanaṁ ca

"I am seated in everyone's heart, and from Me come remembrance, knowledge and forgetfulness." (*Bhagavad-gītā* 15.15)

This is dangerous. If Kṛṣṇa helps us forget Him, watch out! We are going to have a hell of a time (literally).

Dakṣa Loses His Head

In the *Śrīmad-Bhāgavatam*, there is a story about Prajāpati Dakṣa. He did a *yajña* in which all the demigods assembled to honor him. When Dakṣa came to the *yajña* arena, Lord Śiva and Lord Brahmā did not get up to show respects to him. All the other demigods, all the other personalities present there, stood up. Brahmā did not stand up to offer respect to him because Brahmā was his senior, the father of Dakṣa. Lord Śiva, however, was his son-in-law, and Dakṣa expected that Lord Śiva would stand up to offer him worship. At that time, Lord Śiva was deep in meditation. Thus, Dakṣa exploded in anger. He became so upset that he blasphemed Lord Śiva and told him that he will not get any share of the *yajña*. The whole scene then became a mess. Fighting ensued, and Dakṣa physically lost his head. He was eventually brought back to life and his head was replaced with a goat's head (he could still function with human intelligence). He obviously realized that he made a huge mistake and thus apologized to Lord Śiva, even though he had been harboring strong resentment towards Lord Śiva ever since Lord Śiva married his daughter.

In his next life he again took birth as a Prajāpati (progenitor). He gave birth to many sons whom he intended to become Prajāpatis to populate the universe. Nārada Muni preached to his sons the K.I.S.S. principle ("Keep It Simple, *Sādhu*"), and convinced them not to marry. The sons followed his advice, and like any materialistic father, Prajāpati Dakṣa was upset.

However, he tolerated this "transgression".

But the same scenario repeated itself with more of Dakṣa's sons. This time Dakṣa couldn't contain himself, and he cursed Nārada that he would not be able to stay in one place for more than three days.

The *ācāryas* say that because Dakṣa did not fully forgive Lord Śiva in his past life, he carried the remaining vestiges of resentment into his next life. Thus, this resentment again resurfaced and he offended Nārada.

This shows that our desires and aspirations from one life carry over to the next life. Kṛṣṇa causes us to remember desires of the past and continue in that same consciousness in the present life. Why does He do this? Wouldn't it be better for us to start with a clean slate and thus develop a better consciousness? He does this because we want it. Again, we must be careful what we desire.

Kṛṣṇa Gives Intelligence

teṣāṁ satata-yuktānāṁ
bhajatāṁ prīti-pūrvakam
dadāmi buddhi-yogaṁ taṁ
yena mām upayānti te

"To those who are constantly devoted to serving Me with love, I give the understanding by which they can come to Me." (*Bhagavad-gītā* 10.10)

When we want to be Kṛṣṇa conscious, what does Kṛṣṇa do? Kṛṣṇa says *dadāmi buddhi-yogaṁtaṁ* (*Bhagavad-gītā* 10.10) – I give intelligence. Kṛṣṇa can also give us intelligence to give the most "scientifically" astute argument to prove that He does not exist. We could write phenomenally intellectual treatises proving that there is no God. We might even get a Nobel prize for being the most intelligently foolish person in the universe. But *buddhi-yogaṁ* is a different kind of intelligence – the intelligence to connect with Kṛṣṇa.

The Story of Arjunācārya

Once there was a devotee called Arjunācārya. He was very poor. He and his wife had only one piece of cloth that they would wear alternatively whenever they would go out in public, so they could not even go out together. They did not have any food in their house. They used to go out and beg. Sometimes they could not get anything at all. Once, Arjunācārya was reading a verse from the *Bhagavad-gītā*.

ananyāś cintayant omāṁ
ye janāḥ paryupāsate
teṣāṁ nityābhiyuktānāṁ
yoga-kṣemaṁ vahāmy aham

"But those who worship me with exclusive devotion, meditating on My transcendental form – to them I carry what they lack and preserve what they have." (*Bhagavad-gītā* 9.22)

This means if we give ourself to Kṛṣṇa, we don't have to worry how we will live. Kṛṣṇa will take care of us. He will personally deliver what we lack.

While reading this verse, Arjunācārya thought that Kṛṣṇa is not personally coming to my help. He thought that Kṛṣṇa helps through His material energy, but He doesn't personally do it. So he took a red pen and crossed out the lines that say He personally preserves what His devotee has and carries what he lacks.

He then went out for begging. The entire day he could not get anything. While he was out begging, an incredibly beautiful boy and his brother showed up at Arjunācārya's house. They were carrying a stick on their shoulders that held two large baskets filled with grains and vegetables. The boys knocked on the door.

"Mātājī, your husband asked us to bring these groceries to you."

Looking at the small boys carrying all those heavy groceries she said, "How cruel of my husband to ask you to carry all that weight. You are so young."

She then noticed three red lines on the chest of the boy. Worrying about him, she asked, "Can I help you? Are you in pain?"

"Your husband did this to me," the boy replied.

She felt so bad for Him that she invited him in and started cooking for him. While she was cooking, the boy left, knowing that Arjunācārya was coming back. He did not want Arjunācārya to see Him.

When Arjunācārya came back, he saw his wife cooking. He asked her, "Where did you get all this food?"

She said "I got it from the poor boys you sent". How could you be so cruel and ask them to carry such a heavy load?"

"I never sent any boys. What are you talking about?" Arjunācārya said, now confused by what was happening.

"One boy said you asked them to bring the food. He was the one who had three little red marks on His chest. He said you made those marks there."

Arjunācārya realized that the boys were none other than Kṛṣṇa and Balarāma. He went into ecstasy and said, "O Gopīnāth!"

He said to his wife, "Do you realize you just got *darshan* of the Supreme Lord?! How fortunate you are!"

Sincerity Is Our Decision

Now let us go back to the topic of what we control and look at it from another perspective. Sometimes, we may question how much control we have over our own efforts. Once, Śrīla Prabhupāda was asked, "How do we become sincere?" Prabhupāda said, "By being sincere."

So, we actually have control over the degree of sincerity we manifest in our service. We cannot hold somebody else responsible for our lack of sincerity. Sincerity is our decision, our choice to be sincere. Be sincere and Kṛṣṇa will give His mercy.

pārtha naiveha nāmutra
vināśas tasya vidyate
na hi kalyāṇa-kṛt kaścid
durgatiṁ tāta gacchati

"Son of Pṛthā, a transcendentalist engaged in auspicious activities does not meet with destruction either in this world or in the spiritual world; one who does good, My friend, is never overcome by evil." (*Bhagavad-gītā* 6.40)

Here, "doing good" is dependent on our sincerity. It is our sincerity that brings us to Kṛṣṇa consciousness, and it is our sincerity that keeps us in Kṛṣṇa consciousness. Though to be sincere or not to be sincere is our personal choice, the results we get in Kṛṣṇa consciousness are not in our hands.

You cannot force Kṛṣṇa.

There was a devotee who rejected Śrīla Prabhupāda and took shelter of another guru. This devotee wrote a letter to Śrīla Prabhupāda to give justification for leaving Kṛṣṇa consciousness. He said that the real teaching is that we should chant constantly to get *prema*, and he told Prabhupāda without chanting 64 rounds you cannot get *prema*. Prabhupāda replied to his disciples, "You cannot force Kṛṣṇa to give *prema*, even if you are chanting one hundred rounds a day."

We have a choice to be sincere, but we cannot force Kṛṣṇa to produce any specific results. We are dependent on His mercy for the results.

A Temple in Japan

In 1972, Prabhupāda was in Japan, and he wanted to open a temple there. At the time, we had about 30 temples in the world, and Prabhupāda wanted to open 108 temples before he left this world. So opening new temples was important to him. Prabhupāda said, "Whoever opens a temple in Japan, Lord Caitanya will personally come and take them back to Godhead." It is not so easy to go back to Godhead. There are many stages that one must cross in order to attain pure love of God and to realize one's eternal relationship with Kṛṣṇa. Prabhupāda also showed us what is required to go back to Godhead when he said,

"If we have even a little pinch of material desire, we will have to take another birth." So how is it that Prabhupāda is saying that Lord Caitanya will take a devotee back to Godhead when the devotee is not fully qualified?

Opening a new temple in Japan was important to Prabhupāda, yet he didn't want to force anyone to take on this challenge. So he made an amazing offer (which, of course, only he could make). If anyone made the sacrifice to sincerely dedicate themselves to this project, he would be so indebted that he would personally petition Mahāprabhu to take them back to Godhead. This is how mercy works.

No Mercy for the Sannyāsī

Once, a *sannyāsī* wanted to do the *parikramā* of mother Ganges. He went to ask for the permission from his guru, Śrīla Bhaktisiddhānta Sarasvatī Ṭhākura. Although he did not get the permission, he decided to do the *parikramā* anyway. When he returned and informed Śrīla Bhaktisiddhānta that he had done the *parikramā*, Śrīla Bhaktisiddhānta was not pleased and took away his *sannyāsa*. The point is that you cannot get results by doing something that is so-called Kṛṣṇa conscious if it is not pleasing to the one whose mercy you require.

The Japa Tree House

In Māyāpura, there was once a devotee who had attended the Gaura Pūrṇimā festival and wanted to chant 64 rounds a day. To do that, he felt it best to not associate with other devotees as he would be distracted from his *japa*. So he built a tree house on a secluded section of the property and lived and chanted his rounds there. This came to Prabhupāda's attention several times and he finally said something along the lines of as soon as you say "I want," it is *māyā*. So what would he get by chanting 64 rounds a day? According to Prabhupāda, he would get *māyā*.

Our efforts and Kṛṣṇa's mercy both work together. If we are engaged in Kṛṣṇa consciousness wholeheartedly, following the orders of guru and Kṛṣṇa, then Kṛṣṇa will carry what we lack. By mercy, we can do things we normally would not be able to do, and achieve what we normally would be unable to achieve. Devotional service is a partnership.

Act like everything depends on you, and pray like everything depends on God.

CHAPTER 4

Balancing Feelings of Unworthiness

It's common for devotees to feel unqualified or unworthy to serve guru and Kṛṣṇa. This is helpful when it is a natural symptom of spiritual advancement. But it is detrimental when, out of an unhealthy psychology, we either feel unworthy of receiving Kṛṣṇa's grace, or feel unworthy of being loved by Kṛṣṇa. Spiritual unworthiness and material unworthiness are not the same. One is a by-product of a high level of Kṛṣṇa consciousness, and the other is a symptom of an unhealthy mental or emotional state. Is it possible for conditioned souls to develop healthy feelings of unworthiness? If so, what would this look like? And how do we know when those feelings are not Kṛṣṇa conscious but signs of an emotional weakness or problem? We look at these and similar questions in this section.

Isn't It Artificial?

It is an elementary understanding of Kṛṣṇa consciousness that this world is a perverted reflection of the spiritual world. We learn that qualities and characteristics that are undesirable (such as jealousy, anger, sulking, envy, etc.) have their pure, "all-good" spiritual counterparts. What may look like a material defect, or even a mental or emotional illness, can be a symptom of an elevated state of Kṛṣṇa consciousness. Thus, we sometimes see advanced devotees exhibiting extreme lamentation, self-denigration, or hopelessness as aspects of their Kṛṣṇa consciousness.

How are we to relate to this? Can we follow in their footsteps? Is there a kind of lamentation, self-denigration, and hopelessness that's suitable to our level of Kṛṣṇa consciousness? If there is, how can we not become discouraged by such feelings?

Feelings of unworthiness have their place in our lives, and can inspire us if these feelings are genuine and appropriate to our level of Kṛṣṇa consciousness. To come to a level of feeling genuine spiritual unworthiness, we first need to overcome our material feelings of unworthiness. Why? Because these material feelings are not healthy for our *bhakti*.

Let us first look at feelings of unworthiness that are detrimental to our advancement.

Who Is Worthy to Get Kṛṣṇa?

Devotees often feel unworthy to receive Kṛṣṇa's mercy, kindness, and love, feeling that Kṛṣṇa is throwing pearls to a swine. More often than not, such feelings are mixed with, or result from, a material sense of unworthiness (I am bad, I am dirty, I am foolish, I am…). So let's first understand that the Lord doesn't exactly see us as we may see ourselves.

Everybody, by Mahāprabhu's mercy, is worthy of Kṛṣṇa's love and thus worthy to become Kṛṣṇa conscious. How did we all become worthy? What did we do?

Actually, we didn't do anything. All we did was exist. By being a spirit soul (which obviously doesn't take any doing on our part), we are qualified for the Lord's mercy. Mahāprabhu's love is so great that every living being is an object of His affection. Indeed, it is not possible for Him to not love us.

Now, you might say, "Why would Kṛṣṇa care about me? I am insignificant. Besides, I don't even like Kṛṣṇa that much. I try to imitate Him, I neglect Him, I take things from Him, I criticize His devotees, and I always think about my own enjoyment."

Despite all this, Kṛṣṇa always cares about us. How do we know? If He didn't care about us, then why would He empower His holy name with *prema* (i.e.why does He give away *prema* through His holy name)? If Kṛṣṇa didn't want a relationship with us, why did He send so many of His eternal associates to come to this world to bring us back to Him, despite our faults and disqualifications to engage in His service?

If Kṛṣṇa didn't love us, why did He send Śrīla Prabhupāda to go out of his way to save us from our material lives and offer us a one-way ticket to the spiritual world?

This is just a fragment of the evidence that shows how much Kṛṣṇa cares about every one of us. There is nothing we can do, aside from continued blasphemy of, or willing disobedience to Kṛṣṇa's pure devotees, that would make us unworthy of Kṛṣṇa's love. Still, even if we believe we are truly unworthy, this makes us even more qualified to receive His mercy. Just as being poor qualifies one to receive welfare from the government, disqualification is the very cause of being worthy of the Lord's mercy. If Mahāprabhu were selling love of Kṛṣṇa for the price of qualification, He would have closed His shop long ago having gone out of business for lack of customers.

Kṛṣṇa Cares for Every Soul

Abnormal feelings of unworthiness can be caused by being (or feeling) unloved or denigrated by others, or by personal failures in life. In this unhealthy state, we can feel ourselves so low, impure, unintelligent, or unqualified, that even God couldn't find a reason to love us.

A devotee once asked Śrīla Prabhupāda, "Why would Kṛṣṇa care about me? He has so many devotees. He has the *gopīs*, the cowherd boys, His mother and father, and so many servants."

We might feel this way as well. After all, we know we are not perfect and not always Kṛṣṇa conscious. So we can easily think, "Why would Kṛṣṇa care about me? Kṛṣṇa has so many loving devotees and I don't even have a drop of love for Him. Why would He even want to associate with such a lowly person as I?" Prabhupāda explained that if you cut your finger, you try to save it. You don't say to the doctor, "Just let my finger fall off, I have nine other fingers." Similarly, Kṛṣṇa doesn't think, "I have so many other devotees, so who cares about you?" He doesn't think like this because everyone is dear to Kṛṣṇa.

We Give Kṛṣṇa Unique Pleasure

Viśvanātha Cakravartī Ṭhākura describes that every living entity has a unique relationship with Kṛṣṇa, and thus Kṛṣṇa experiences unique pleasure from every individual relationship. In other words, Kṛṣṇa relishes a unique taste from His relationship with every one of us. This means He is anxious to taste that specific *rāsa* with each of us. Not only that, He has a unique way of reciprocating with each one of us; a unique taste that He offers to each and every relationship.

So it's not that Kṛṣṇa is ambivalent about us. He very much wants a relationship with us, so much so that He is actively trying to get us back into that relationship. The problem is not that Kṛṣṇa doesn't care about the relationship; the difficulty only comes when we don't care enough about the relationship. This means, the problem is not that Kṛṣṇa feels we are unworthy of a relationship; the problem is we don't feel worthy of the relationship.

(This may also mean that feelings of unworthiness are sometimes excuses we make to ourselves to avoid properly working on our relationship with Kṛṣṇa.)

We Are Misunderstanding Kṛṣṇa's Affection

If somebody gives us a gift, we might feel unworthy of accepting it, but out of respect, and to reciprocate affection, we accept the gift nonetheless. After all, it would be rude not to accept someone's expression of love for us because we feel unworthy of it. Similarly, Kṛṣṇa gives us the gift of Himself in His holy name, in the spiritual master, in the *saṅga* of devotees, in His temples, through His *arcā-mūrti* – in so many ways. It is a rejection of His affection to say, "No, I am not going to accept these gifts because I am not worthy of them." If we did say that, Kṛṣṇa would reply, "It doesn't matter that you are not qualified. I am giving you Myself. Being worthy isn't My criteria. I give Myself to you, not because you are worthy, but because I love you." So it's not a question of whether or not we are worthy. It comes down to receiving Kṛṣṇa's love.

Kṛṣṇa is called Rasarāja, the king of relationships. Kṛṣṇa thrives on relationships, and if Kṛṣṇa wants a relationship with us, we can't deny Him by saying, "No, just don't expect much reciprocation from me because I'm not worthy of a relationship with You."Are we so foolish as to say to Kṛṣṇa, "I am unavailable to you?"

Stop Putzing Around

There is an expression in Yiddish called "putzing." If someone is "putzing around" it means they are being busy doing a lot of useless activities that amount to nothing. "Putzing around" basically means, as Bob Dylan sang, "Being busy doing nothing."

We are all very busy in the material world doing millions of things that ultimately amount to nothing more than preparing for our next birth. In other words, we tend to be expert at "putzing around." Have you ever been in a rush to make an appointment and you call for one of your family members to get in the car, but they are holding you up by being busy doing nothing of much consequence? In the same way, Kṛṣṇa is calling us to leave this world because we are "putzing around" here, doing a million unimportant things that amount only to holding Him up.

Kṛṣṇa is saying, "I've got a place for you in My home. Your spiritual body is ready for you; your service is ready for you; all arrangements are there for your eternal stay. Stop 'putzing around' and come back home!"

Kṛṣṇa Is Waiting for Us

In Māyāpura, Jananivasa Prabhu said in a class that it seems awkward that Mādhava (Māyāpura's Deity) is playing His flute because Kṛṣṇa plays His flute to call Rādhārāṇī and the *gopīs*. Since Rādhārāṇī and the *gopīs* are already there (on the altar in Māyāpura), Kṛṣṇa doesn't need to play the flute. So why is He playing it? He's playing His flute to call us. His flute sings a song that goes something like this: "Come home. I am waiting for you. Stop 'putzing around.' What are you doing that's so important?"

At the end of a class I once gave at a college in India, the Dean of the college expressed his feelings thusly, "What's the problem if I stay in the material world life after life if I am happy? I do good *karma*, serve others, and don't hurt anybody."

I told him, "Kṛṣṇa wants you to come back to Him. He's waiting for you." I could sense that he appreciated this answer. Later that evening he enthusiastically told me, "You made me realize that Kṛṣṇa is waiting for me."

This is how we should also think. Thoughts of being worthy or not are simply getting in the way of the real fact that Kṛṣṇa is waiting for us.

Do You Want to Dance With Kṛṣṇa?

Śrīla Prabhupāda would often end his lectures with encouraging words. Sometimes he would say that one day you will see Kṛṣṇa face to face just like we are seeing one another. At other times he would say that someday you will dance with Kṛṣṇa. When Śrīla Prabhupāda makes promises like this, we shouldn't say, "Yeah but not me. I am too useless. I am not worthy or qualified." That translates into, "Nah, I'll just be staying down here putzing around. That's all I am good for."

Kṛṣṇa is waiting to dance with us. What fools we are to make excuses not to join the dance?

The All-Attractive Tries to Attract Us

Kṛṣṇa didn't have to come to the material world. Yet He came and performed His *līlās* to attract us back to Him. In fact, everything that Kṛṣṇa does is ultimately done for this purpose. In other words, He only acts to help us re-establish our relationship with Him. He creates the material world to give us a chance to reform ourselves and He performs His pastimes to attract our mind and heart to Him. This means He performs His pastimes to awaken our love for Him. Try to feel this affection when you hear His *līlās* and try to feel Him calling you into a relationship with Him. When you read between the lines of the *Śrīmad-Bhāgavatam*, you can hear Kṛṣṇa saying, "Please accept My love. Please join Me in My eternal *līlā*."

Kṛṣṇa Attracts Us Through His Devotees

Similarly, when reading Śrīla Prabhupāda's purports, behind the words you can feel Prabhupāda showering love and compassion. Of course, the message of the purport is there, but behind the message, allow yourself to feel the love that Śrīla Prabhupāda has for you and me, and all conditioned souls.

Prabhupāda's love for us is further evidence of Kṛṣṇa's love for us. Prabhupāda is a messenger of Kṛṣṇa's love, and thus he loves us all without discrimination. Prabhupāda loves everyone to such a degree that he never rejects anyone, no matter how fallen, who is willing to serve Kṛṣṇa.

Positive Unworthiness

Still, as stated earlier, there are proper feelings of unworthiness appropriate to our level of advancement. These feelings are both natural and helpful for *bhakti*. So what are these natural feelings for neophyte devotees and how do they manifest?

Feelings of unworthiness manifest in two prominent ways in the stage of *vaidhī-sādhana-bhakti*: appreciation and humility. Appreciation manifests in gratitude that Kṛṣṇa accepts us and our service despite our past sins and present faults as long as we simply make a sincere effort to serve Him and Śrīla Prabhupāda. Even though unqualified, Kṛṣṇa mercifully gives us lots of service. As we meditate on how Kṛṣṇa allows us, even though unqualified, to be engaged in His service, our appreciation for Him and the service He gives us grows. Thus, feelings of unworthiness help us see our service as a precious gift that we are blessed to have.

Feeling unworthy also makes us feel helpless. Taken in the correct way, helplessness is a manifestation of humility in accordance with our present level of Kṛṣṇa consciousness. It manifests as a total dependence on Kṛṣṇa for guidance, intelligence, and ability to do our service well – or sometimes even to do our service at all. It is through this kind of humility that we advance rapidly in Kṛṣṇa consciousness. Thus, feelings of unworthiness, when exhibited in a Kṛṣṇa conscious sense, become one of our greatest allies in *sādhana-bhakti*, because humility is integral to advancing in Kṛṣṇa consciousness.

The Bottom Line

So yes, we should feel unworthy. We don't deserve Kṛṣṇa's love. We are not qualified to even be a devotee. We have turned our back on Kṛṣṇa, we have competed with Him, we have disobeyed Him, and we have even tried to become like Him.

Still, Kṛṣṇa overlooks all of this and forgives us. His desire for a relationship with us is so strong that He will not allow any of this to get in the way. As Kṛṣṇa will not allow our own disqualifications to get in the way, we should also never allow our own disqualifications to get in our way. Rather, we should allow our feelings of unworthiness to bring us closer and closer to Kṛṣṇa. This is what Kṛṣṇa wants us to do.

In the *Bṛhad-bhāgavatāmṛta*, when Gopa Kumar arrives in the spiritual world and first meets Kṛṣṇa, the Lord tells him, "Why did you take so long? Why did you make me wait so long for you? I missed you so much."

Yes, Kṛṣṇa does miss us. Let's stop putzing around. Kṛṣṇa is waiting for us.

CHAPTER 5

Balancing Taste and Sense Gratification

Is it wrong to want to taste Kṛṣṇa? Wouldn't that desire be sense gratification? Shouldn't we just serve without any personal desire? These are important questions to address.

There is a difference between taste in Kṛṣṇa consciousness and sense gratification, although they can seem similar, and thus difficult to distinguish. We discuss this difference, as well as the necessity of developing the proper taste for Kṛṣṇa consciousness.

The Goal Is to Gratify Kṛṣṇa's Senses

What is the motive behind sense gratification? It is simply to squeeze the maximum amount of pleasure out of our senses. This is the sum and substance of material life. It is also the sum and substance of animal life.

Our senses are also gratified in Kṛṣṇa consciousness, but there's a huge difference in the motive with which we engage our senses.

When a devotee reaches higher levels of Kṛṣṇa consciousness, he is not focused on what will or will not make him happy. His only thoughts are how to make Kṛṣṇa, his gurus, and the devotees happy, and how to give Kṛṣṇa consciousness to others. In this way, a devotee never considers his personal happiness.

There Must Be Anxiety for Kṛṣṇa

Non-devotees are often in a state of anxiety thinking, "Will this work out, will that work out?" These anxieties are, of course, related to personal well-being. A devotee, however, is never in a state of anxiety about his personal life. Rather, his only anxiety is whether things will work out for Kṛṣṇa's service. This is the real stress relief formula. Once you stop worrying about yourself and start worrying about making guru, Kṛṣṇa, and others happy, your material anxieties will be gone.

Devotees once wanted to buy a huge church in Toronto to convert into a temple. Since it was very expensive, Śrīla Prabhupāda told them not to get it because, "You'll be buying anxiety." When Prabhupāda later returned to Toronto, he asked the temple president if he purchased the temple. The temple president said, "No, since it is so expensive we would be buying anxiety." Amazingly, Prabhupāda strongly replied, "There must be anxiety for Kṛṣṇa. Otherwise, there will simply be anxiety for sense gratification." So all of our anxiety should be in relation to how we can best serve Kṛṣṇa and help others come to Kṛṣṇa consciousness.

Hanker After Pleasing Guru and Kṛṣṇa

When we get a taste for Kṛṣṇa, we no longer hanker for material tastes, and thus we stop being self-centered. Therefore, the intelligent question is, "How can we get a taste for Kṛṣṇa?" We get a taste for Kṛṣṇa by not trying to taste *māyā*. It is only when we are hankering to please guru and Kṛṣṇa, and not calculating what will or will not make us happy, that we become happy in Kṛṣṇa consciousness. (This is different from considering basic needs that must be fulfilled.)

"There is another wonderful feature of the emotion of the *gopīs*. Its power is beyond the comprehension of the intelligence. When the *gopīs* see Lord Kṛṣṇa, they derive unbounded bliss, although they have no desire for such pleasure. The *gopīs* taste a pleasure ten million times greater than the pleasure Lord Kṛṣṇa derives from seeing them." (*Śrī Caitanya-caritāmṛta, Ādi-līlā* 4.185-87)

Sense Gratification – An Addiction

Taste is a by-product of pleasing Kṛṣṇa's senses. Therefore, we should never run away from trying to gain a genuine taste in Kṛṣṇa consciousness, thinking it to be sense gratification. Taste in Kṛṣṇa consciousness is very different from the taste of sense gratification. One comes as a by-product of purified senses and the other as a by-product of lust.

"This taste is the seed of devotional service, and one who is fortunate enough to have received such a seed is advised to sow it in the core of his heart." (*Śrīmad-Bhāgavatam* 3.2.6, Purport)

"I see that you have acquired a taste for hearing talks regarding Kṛṣṇa. Therefore you are extremely fortunate. Not only you but anyone who has awakened such a taste is considered most fortunate." (*Śrī Caitanya-caritāmṛta, Antya-līlā* 5.9)

Tasting Is the Secret of Success

Taste for Kṛṣṇa is juxtaposed to sense gratification. When we are hankering after sensual pleasure, or particularly when we are engaged in it, the so-called pleasure we get nullifies our senses' ability to perceive, or desire, pleasure in Kṛṣṇa consciousness. Conversely, a higher taste in Kṛṣṇa consciousness nullifies the taste for sense gratification. When our taste for Kṛṣṇa is strong, we will be disgusted to even think about past sense gratification. The very things that we used to hanker for, the things we used to love to do, eat, hear, talk about, see, etc., will become distasteful.

Devotees often ask me, "How will I know if I am making advancement?" You know you are advancing when material life becomes distasteful. Taste counteracts the desire for sense gratification. Thus, Śrīla Prabhupāda tells us that taste is the "secret of success."

Māyā – The Attractive Energy of the All-Attractive

The problem is that since Kṛṣṇa is all-attractive, His external energy, *māyā*, is also attractive (after all, it is His energy). Śrīla Prabhupāda said that *māyā* means that other things become more attractive than Kṛṣṇa.

I was listening to a conversation in which a devotee was telling Śrīla Prabhupāda how some priests have girlfriends, get married, or become homosexuals. It was even common for some priests to become alcoholics. Prabhupāda replied, "Yes, they must fall down because they are not getting a taste." So without Kṛṣṇa, we are guaranteed to be attracted by *māyā*, even if we don't want to be, and even if we try hard not to be. We do not "fight *māyā*" simply with discipline. We fight *māyā* through the taste that engagement in Kṛṣṇa consciousness gives us.

"The more the taste grows, the more one desires to render service to the Lord." (*Śrī Caitanya-caritāmṛta, Madhya-līlā* 23.13, Purport)

Anarthas Won't Make Us Happy

We are unfortunate if we believe anything outside of Kṛṣṇa consciousness will give us a taste in life. The irony is that the stage of *ruci* (or taste for Kṛṣṇa), which gives us real happiness and pleasure, comes after material desires are given up. In other words, the material things we think will make us happy are actually the very things that prevent us from being happy.

Planting the Seed of Bhakti in Others

Śrīla Prabhupāda once said in a letter written on January 10, 1972, "Our business is simply to plant the seed of devotional service wherever we go, and to give everyone a taste of this transcendentally relishable activity of life." If people get a transcendental experience, or taste, it will be a huge faith builder for them because they will experience pleasure beyond the senses. And when people get a taste for Kṛṣṇa, they will want more.

In the *Śrī Caitanya-caritāmṛta* it is said that Mahāprabhu tasted the fruits of love of God, and then distributed those fruits.

"He taught everyone how to taste the transcendental mellow ecstasy of love of Kṛṣṇa by tasting it Himself." (*Śrī Caitanya-caritāmṛta, Ādi-līlā* 13.39)

Purification for Taste

Taste comes by purification of the senses. Kṛṣṇa is tasteful, and only purified senses can taste Kṛṣṇa. In the *Harinama Cintāmaṇi*, it is said, "When one's heart is purified, one's interest and taste for culturing *bhakti* begins."

It is essential that we understand taste as an experience that results from relishing Kṛṣṇa consciousness with purified senses, and that taste has nothing to do with material motivation. Taste is something all great devotees hanker for. Even the Lord Himself hankers for it.

"What to speak of others, even Kṛṣṇa, the son of Nanda Mahārāja, personally descends to taste the nectar of love of Godhead in the form of the chanting of Hare Kṛṣṇa." (*Śrī Caitanya-caritāmṛta, Antya-līlā* 3.265)

Monitoring the Taste-O-Meter

In one lecture, Śrīla Prabhupāda was asked, "How do you monitor whether or not you're becoming Kṛṣṇa conscious?" His response was, "By your detachment. By your freedom from sex desire." Caitanya Mahāprabhu says, "How do you know an advanced devotee? You know by his taste for the holy name."

If we see ourselves becoming more inclined and attracted to Kṛṣṇa, we are on the right track. However, if we see ourselves becoming more attracted to mundane things, we should understand something is wrong. So taste is a useful meter with which to monitor our advancement.

"Therefore, one's development of a taste for executing these instructions is the test of one's devotional service." (*Śrī Caitanya-caritāmṛta, Ādi-līlā* 1.60, Purport)

And what is the result of chanting without taste? Bhaktivinoda Ṭhākura answers this question in the *Harinama Cintāmaṇi*:

"Though chanting *japa* daily, if his taste is elsewhere, he will show indifference to the name. His heart will not be absorbed in chanting the name but in some material object. How can that benefit him? He may chant 64 rounds counting strictly on his *japa* beads, but in his heart he has not received one drop of the taste of the name. This indifference or apathy towards the name is one type of inattention. In the heart of a materialist it is unavoidable."

Riding Downhill

Ruci is compared to riding downhill because in this stage of Kṛṣṇa consciousness we are motivated by a taste to serve, not by rules and regulations. Before we have a taste, we must make a constant effort to control ourselves. At the stage of *ruci*, such efforts are not required since our taste for Kṛṣṇa is the motivating factor. As the saying goes, "It is all downhill from here."

Don't Run Away From Taste

If you have the idea in your mind that, "I shouldn't want taste," understand that we'll always be motivated by taste. So it's just a question of what kind of taste will motivate us. Just as material taste is drawing us closer to *māyā*, spiritual taste is drawing us closer to Kṛṣṇa.

"To taste the fruit of devotional service in Goloka Vṛndāvana is the highest perfection of life, and in the presence of such perfection, the four material perfections — religion, economic development, sense gratification and liberation — are very insignificant achievements. (*Śrī Caitanya-caritāmṛta, Madhya-līlā* 19.164)

We should want taste, pray for taste, and hanker for taste. We need taste.

"When one is so situated that he can taste the association of Lord Kṛṣṇa, material existence, the repetition of birth and death, comes to an end." (*Śrī Caitanya-caritāmṛta, Madhya-līlā* 20.141)

What Are You Afraid Of?

Don't be afraid of tasting Kṛṣṇa consciousness. Be afraid of enjoying Kṛṣṇa consciousness. We want to serve Kṛṣṇa, not enjoy Kṛṣṇa. The paradox is that if we serve, we end up enjoying Kṛṣṇa consciousness. Kṛṣṇa consciousness is not derived from the desire to enjoy. Indeed, it is pleasure of service that removes the desire to enjoy.

We Are Ordered to Relish Kṛṣṇa consciousness

Perfection is to taste the nectar of Kṛṣṇa consciousness.

"The nectar from the lips of Lord Kṛṣṇa and His transcendental qualities and characteristics surpass the taste of the essence of all nectar, and there is no fault in tasting such nectar. If one does not taste it, he should die immediately after birth, and his tongue is to be considered no better than the tongue of a frog." (*Śrī Caitanya-caritāmṛta, Madhya-līlā* 2.32)

CHAPTER 6

Just Do It

I apologize in advance for the length of this section. The information I offer goes very deep into a part of our psychology that is not easily understood (or not easily accepted). Thus, I needed more space to ensure that the message, and its application, would be clear.

This chapter outlines one of the foundational points for a workshop I developed called the Re-Creation Workshop. The workshop deals with understanding our psychological conditioning from the Vedantic perspective and using the knowledge to live in alignment with our ideals.

This chapter can do much to help you deal with ways of thinking and behaving that you would like to change. I suggest reading it several times. The message is simple, but since it is simple it can easily be taken as "I know that." My experience is that much of what we know is not deeply engrained within us. My hope is that this will implant what we know a little deeper in our hearts and thus make it come alive.

So what is this section about? It is about deeper levels of our material conditioning that appear virtually impossible to overcome – and how to deal with this.

We all deal with our "demons," and despite repeated attempts, we often fail to overcome – or even keep at bay – some of our most deeply seated anarthas. So we continue in hopes that our anarthas will eventually be cleansed by the process of sādhana-bhakti. Yet, after years of practice, when some anarthas still have their grip on us, we naturally question whether we will ever overcome them in this life.

In this section, we look at a solution to this problem that is so simple that it escapes many of us. And we then analyze this solution according to the modes of nature.

Stick with the chapter to the end. It will be well worth your time.

The Solution Is in Your Hands

Some internal problems we face are persistent. They remain with us, to one degree or another, despite repeated attempts to resolve them, or even after we think they have been resolved. Thus, it is common to feel there is little we can do about such *anarthas*.

There is a simple solution, but it is not simplistic. Profound truths are almost always simple. Yet, because they are simple, they are often overlooked, ignored, or even scoffed at.

Prabhupāda said, "Kṛṣṇa consciousness is so simple you can miss it."

The solution I suggest is commitment.

In most cases, our problems persist because we are not deeply committed to overcoming them. (There are reasons for this, and we will discuss them later on).

Your first reaction might be, "That is too easy. It cannot work for my problems. Some of my *anarthas* have been pulling me around for years."

You might think that your problems require a thorough analysis of their cause, and a detailed, long-term and rigorous step-by-step process to overcome them. Granted, in some cases this is true, but it is my experience that these are the exceptions, and are usually cases in which there has been severe emotional damage or trauma.

In the majority of cases, willpower reigns supreme. In my counseling work, I find that almost everyone underestimates the strength of their own willpower. Thus, they don't realize that solutions are almost always within their own hands. It is like we are denying that we have free will. (Excuses are normally an erroneous attempt to prove that we can't do anything about a situation).

Just Be Sincere

When Prabhupāda was asked how to become sincere, he replied, "By being sincere." He went on to explain that you become a drunkard by drinking, or a thief by stealing, so you become sincere by being sincere. In other words, you take it upon yourself to do your bhakti sincerely.

"Well, Prabhu, how can I just be sincere? I mean, how do you do that?"

"You just do it."

"Is that all there is to it?"

"Yes."

"That's too simple."

"That's the point!"

Another time he said if you don't feel like dancing in the *kirtan*, dance anyway.

"Prabhu, how do you do that? I mean, how can you do something joyous like dancing in a kirtan if you are feeling miserable?"

Step 1: Stand up.
Step 2: Move your feet.
Step 3: Raise your hands.
Step 4: Jump up and down.
Step 5: Chant Hare Kṛṣṇa.

That's all there is to it. That's not that difficult, is it?

By the way, if you do that, you probably won't feel miserable for long. If you act in a certain way, even though the action has no correlation to your mentality, the action will change your mentality. As Prabhupāda said, "Bow down even if you don't feel like it, and by doing so, you will feel like bowing down."

I Do Not See the Way Out of Here

We often psyche ourselves out by thinking we cannot overcome a problem when the only thing stopping us is our lack of commitment, our lack of just doing it. We often get caught in the trap of thinking that the problem is so deep, or so complex, that we cannot imagine a way out of it.

Here is a typical example: Many devotees tell me they would like to get up early, but are unable to do it. So they ask me, "How can I get up early?"

By now you might be able to guess what I tell them.

"Just get up early."

Most devotees don't expect – or even want – that answer. I think they want a magic bullet: a mantra, a magic potion, or a *Mahātmā-sūtra* that just gets them up early. Or perhaps they thought I could tell them where to buy a mystic mattress that automatically gets them up at their desired time.

Nothing just gets us up early. We get ourselves up early.

Do You Really Want It?

If you really want to get up early, you can do it, even without an alarm clock. Of course, "if you really want to," is the key. When asking yourself how to do anything that has been difficult for you to do, ask if you really want it. If you do not really want it, you will find great difficulty committing to it.

"If you don't get what you want, it's a sign either that you did not seriously want it, or that you tried to bargain over the price." (Rudyard Kipling)

This is a simple point; so simple that we sometimes miss it. Let's see how this works in real life.

In my forgiveness workshop, I ask the question, "If Kṛṣṇa offered to remove your resentment immediately, would you take up His offer?" You might think everyone would answer yes.

Not everyone does. Many hesitate because they believe their offender does not deserve their forgiveness. I ask this question to demonstrate that if they are reluctant to forgive, I won't be able to help them much. Nothing I say, and not even the forgiveness processes I offer them, will work unless they are open, in principle, to allowing the resentment to go. If they are unwilling to "let go," they "just won't do it" despite the many good reasons to forgive.

Of course, often we require "many good reasons" to bring us to the point of committing. Thus, knowledge is often an important – or even essential – ingredient in the commitment process. Or we require good association to increase our motivation. Yet, the "I know I should, but..." syndrome is a serious and pervasive disease. You can lead a horse to water but...you know the rest of the story.

By the way, knowledge of what and why you should do something causes increased misery when you don't do it. "I know I should, but..." is not a happy mantra. So, if you don't know what you are supposed to be doing, you won't regret not doing it. "Ignorance is bliss" does have some useful applications.

Rise and Shine

Let's look at the problem of knowing what to do and apply it to getting up early.

Let's say I came up with a workshop on rising early. We'll call it "The Early Bird Workshop." In this workshop I am going to give attendees every good reason under the sun (I mean, under the moon) to get up early. Plus, I will offer them every possible technique to get their bodies upright and their eyes open before the sun rises, including offering a device that automatically turns their lights and stereo on at 4 a.m. Plus, I will have a selection of CDs for early rising that include such sounds as *brahmāstra* weapons exploding, dogs, jackals, and coyotes howling, and a heavy metal band playing out-of-tune guitars and singing completely off key. I mean that ought to get them up, right?

Sounds like a great workshop to me.

Do you think everyone in the workshop will become an early riser for the rest of their life? Most will start rising earlier for a while, but only those who commit will stay with it. If you have attended my *Japa* workshop, you know by now that the most important thing you can do to chant well is commit to good *japa* on a daily basis. Trying to build a good *japa* practice with the blocks of wisdom you receive at a workshop only works when built on the foundation of commitment.

Those who decide that getting up early is what they are going to do, come hell or high water, won't need the workshop or those nasty CDs. In fact, they won't even need an alarm clock! They'll just get up. Hey, if this book goes viral, it will put the alarm clock industry out of business!

That's It

"So, why can't I just do it? I mean I want to do it and I know I should do it, so what's holding me back?" It may be because there is something you are getting from the anartha. Maybe you get some form of pleasure, comfort, or satisfaction. Maybe you get control or ego gratification. *Māyā* is such a good magician that she makes us think that maintaining *anarthas* is a source of pleasure. If we think like this, rather than committing to overcoming *anarthas*, we keep them well fed and protected. Although they are *anartha* (without value), we see them as *artha* (with value).

If you think this might be true in your case, make a list of what you are getting from your *anarthas* and what it is costing you to maintain it. I trust you will realize that the costs don't justify the benefits.

"The price of discipline is less than the pain of regret." (Nido Qubein)

The sad truth is we usually don't realize there is something we are getting from our *anarthas* that we are unwilling to give up. When this happens, it is common to justify our weakness with numerous disempowering arguments and slogans. We assert a weakness or disability as an excuse and thus we 'succeed' by failing. Of course, this doesn't change our behavior, but it does a good job at subduing guilt.

I was once contemplating a strategy to overcome a persistent problem. As I thought about my situation, I realized that I have an attachment that is so deeply rooted within my being that if I just do not say, "That's it, we are finished with this," this attachment will endlessly continue to get the best of me. Yes, *bhakti* does produce detachment, but unless we are sufficiently detaching ourselves from unfavorable thoughts and actions, we won't be practicing *bhakti* well enough for it to completely and naturally eradicate our attachments at their core.

So sometimes all we need is this one little mantra "That's it!"to put an end to an attachment that never seems to stop bothering us. It is a powerful mantra. Think of something right now you would like to throw this mantra at.

Okay, did you think of it?

Now tell yourself, "That's it! I am done giving this *anartha* any more energy."

The Modes

Looking at our discussion from the perspective of the modes of nature is helpful. "I know I should, but..." is a textbook description of the mode of ignorance. In the mode of ignorance, determination doesn't go beyond the dreaming or contemplation stage.

Passion is different. Passion says, "You need to get more done." You thus stay up late trying to get everything done, and trying to finish the rounds you couldn't finish during your busy day. You don't necessarily sleep too much, you just stay up late to get as much done as you can. Since you then rise late the next morning, soon after you rise, you start feeling the pressure of daytime. Thus, you find it difficult to concentrate on your chanting.

Although you know this is wrong, passion won't let you slow down. Thus, again you'll work late into the evening, knock off your last rounds half asleep, and get up late the next morning. Sometimes, you jump on your computer or smart phone to check your messages and e-mail right after you get up. You know this is wrong, but... Passion is the enemy of the mantra "That's it! I've had enough." In passion, the hope and optimism to keep achieving covers any acknowledgment that this activity is not working for me, for my family, or for my spiritual life. In passion we never say, "Since it is not making me happy, since it is not helping me, since it's not in alignment with *bhakti*, I should give it up." In passion, we say, "I can still do it all, but I will get more serious about *bhakti* and I will simplify my life." But this never happens.

This change only happens when you come to goodness.

Goodness is the platform from which you can choose to act the way you prefer. It is the "I know I should, and I will do it" platform of existence. You determine right goals, determine right ways to reach them, and then perform those right actions. "Just Do It" is the textbook mantra of goodness.

So when *śāstra* tells us such things as, "Be enthusiastic," "Be patient," or, "Be tolerant," they are appealing to us to act in goodness. Otherwise, in passion or ignorance, it doesn't seem possible that we can just do something simply because it is the right thing to do. And it is from passion and ignorance that we hit a dead end and helplessly ask such questions as, "How do I get out of this mess?" "How do I improve?" "How do I change?" or make the excuse (which we think is an astute observation) that we can't "just do it." Ignorance and passion are full of excuses that are logical only to the persons making them.

You Have the Power

The attitude and understanding that we have the power to deal with or overcome many difficult problems or obstacles makes a huge difference in our lives. Prabhupāda clearly expressed this mood and understanding whenever he was told that some devotees were having difficulty following their initiation vows.

(Initiation vows is a big topic and I am not addressing it here since I have addressed vows in the chapter titled, "*No One Can Change You the Way You Can.*" My intention is not to condemn those who cannot follow their vows perfectly, but to help all of us understand that we can do more to follow than we often think we can.)

When told that some devotees were not chanting their rounds, Prabhupāda asked if they were eating and sleeping. He said that if they cannot finish their rounds, then they should reduce the time they spend for eating or sleeping in order to make time to finish their rounds. In other words, Prabhupāda is saying if you are committed to finishing your rounds, you will do whatever it takes to keep your vow.

Prabhupāda's response to devotees who were being tossed around by difficulties was often in the mood of, "Why are you allowing yourself to fall into this condition?"

Apply the Process

Let's apply what we are learning. Think of something you are doing that you would like to stop doing, or something you are not doing that you would like to start doing (or do more of), and write it down.

Good. Here's what I want you to do.

On your mark.

Get set.

Go!

Commit to doing what you just wrote down!

You've Done It Before

You can do this. You've done it before. You made a huge commitment when you became serious about Kṛṣṇa consciousness. You added new activities to your life and stopped old ones. How did you do this? You simply decided, "This is what I am going to do." With this attitude, and despite the odds against you, you just did it. Even sex and drug-crazed hippies became *sādhus*, sometimes in a matter of days. This clearly demonstrates the power of "just do it" coupled with the process of *bhakti* and the mercy of guru and Kṛṣṇa.

But I Am Not the Controller

Now you might say, "But Prabhu, it sounds like you are saying we are in control – that we can do whatever we set our minds to. That sounds materialistic. That is not our philosophy. We are totally dependent on Kṛṣṇa for our success."

You are right, but it is a qualified "right."

Once, a devotee asked Prabhupāda if it was okay to pray to Kṛṣṇa to overcome her problems. Prabhupāda said, "Yes, you can pray if you also act to overcome the problems." In other words, self-discipline is exactly what the words describe – you control yourself. So where does Kṛṣṇa come in? He gives us the strength and determination we require to overcome our problems. However, before He does this, we must first commit. As Prabhupāda often said, Kṛṣṇa did not tell Arjuna to go to sleep, and that He would do everything. No. Kṛṣṇa said you must fight, and then I will do everything.

Kṛṣṇa will run with you, but He won't run for you. We require a level of faith that speaks to our heart that, "I can do this because Kṛṣṇa will help me." Do you think it's difficult for Kṛṣṇa to get you up early in the morning? He can lift Govardhana Hill with His pinky, so getting you out of bed is a breeze for Him. But He is not even going to try if you don't sincerely want His help. So all we have to do is want something badly enough to attract Kṛṣṇa's attention. Then, if Kṛṣṇa helps us, we have nothing to worry about.

I Committed. The Problem Is Still There

A common scenario is that you commit, yet the *anartha* remains. When you commit, it does not always mean that the *anartha* goes away. It is Kṛṣṇa's business to purify you of *anarthas*, in His own time, according to your application of the process of *bhakti*. The *anarthas* are purified on different levels of *bhakti*. It is up to you to properly apply the process of *bhakti*, but it is up to Kṛṣṇa when you reach those higher levels of Kṛṣṇa consciousness.

What you do have control of right now is the power *anarthas* have over you. Your commitment is to refuse to be subservient to the demands of your *anarthas*. As you commit, the intensity of the problems the *anartha* causes you subsides.

"As long as one has the material body, the demands of the body for sense gratification will continue. The devotee, however, is not disturbed by such desires, because of his fullness." (*Bhagavad-gītā* 2.70)

This is really just the ABCs of *bhakti*, but somehow, we often forget this simple truth and become discouraged by the presence of unwanted desires in our heart.

Once, a devotee said to Prabhupāda, "It's difficult to control my tongue." Prabhupāda said, "I know, I also have a tongue," indicating that the pushing and pulling of the senses exist for all who have a material body. The important point is how you deal with it.

This could be a topic for an entire chapter. The ability to resist falling prey to, or becoming discouraged by, the presence of material desires, is essential for remaining enthusiastic in devotional service, despite the "valid reasons" to be discouraged.

Now maybe you are saying, "Yeah, this all sounds good, but..."

Oh no, the "but" word again. You know what you are doing to yourself when you say "but?" You are giving yourself all the good reasons why you must fail. You are building a case for why you cannot do something. I guess this makes sense if you don't want to do it and you need a dose of self-pity. In that case, "but" is quite useful.

Hopefully, you don't live in these dark regions of consciousness. Still, it is important to look a little further at what "but" means.

"But" is an argument for your limitations, and when you argue for your limitations, you get to keep those limitations. "But" will cause you to procrastinate, to hide behind fear, and come up with all kinds of excuses to validate inaction.

"But" is a paralyzing word and a classic mode of ignorance response.

Many devotees say, "But I tried a few times and it did not work out." They then use this as an excuse to stop trying. Don't worry. If at first you don't succeed, you are normal. Success comes after many failures. Every master was first a disaster. Moreover, you won't fail unless you give up.

Just do it. No one else is going to do it for you.

If you still have doubts, remember this: Your life gets better when you get better, and nothing gets better if you don't get better.

Do Something

Before we end this section, I have one request. Please commit to something you know you should be doing, or doing better, and experience for yourself the power of "just do it." You can start with something as simple as committing to totally absorb yourself in one round a day, or reading one verse of *śāstra* every day. Just commit to something so you can begin strengthening the "muscle" that enables you to determine what you want to do and allows you to do it, and that prevents you from being a puppet in the hands of the modes of nature. In other words, your mind, senses, and emotions control your life when you (as in spirit soul) don't.

Don't spend half your life telling others what you are going to do and the other half explaining why you didn't do it.

Afterthoughts

Before releasing this chapter, I posted my advice to "just do it" on Facebook, and much discussion followed. As I said, some felt this was too simplistic a solution, while others said they already apply this solution with great success. One devotee said he applied this strategy to overcome his addiction to alcohol.

After reflecting on this exchange, I concluded that Kṛṣṇa's instruction to, "Just surrender unto Me," is really another way of saying, "just do it." Of course, it took convincing to bring Arjuna to this position, and Kṛṣṇa brought Arjuna step-by-step to the point of accepting His will. Yet, by saying "surrender" Kṛṣṇa is telling Arjuna to forget the step-by-step process and just go for it. To me, this kind of surrender is like diving into a river on a cold morning as opposed to going in the river step-by-step. The goal is the same, but one takes a lot longer to get to the same place. In other words, in the end, we still have to dunk our head under the water.

Kṛṣṇa said "surrender," and Arjuna finally did. He picked up his weapons and fought like anything.

Arjuna won the war, regained his kingdom, pleased Kṛṣṇa, and became purified, showing us that great power comes by following the words of guru and Kṛṣṇa. So let us never underestimate the power of "just do it."

Which also proves that Nike was right all along.

SECTION FOUR

Mini Japa Course

CHAPTER 1

Building Your Foundation

There are ten installments in this japa course. I suggest that you focus on one or two installments per week, integrating what you have learned into your japa that week.

At the end of each installment, write down the realizations you get by applying the practices. Writing your realizations will help you to better imbibe what you are learning, and also serve you in the future as a reminder of the realizations you were getting while doing this course.

Evaluating Your Japa

On a scale of 1 to 10, rate how your *japa* has been in the recent past.

Consider what you can do to improve and start to implement these ideas. Regularly monitor the quality of your *japa* by considering what is going well, what isn't going well, and how you can improve.

Little improvements over time amount to major progress.

Without making a regular effort to improve, our *japa* can easily lapse into a mediocre state. If we are not trying to regularly improve, it can easily get worse.

The difference between offensive chanting and the clearing stage, is the effort you make to improve. When you make your best effort, you are at least on the clearing stage.

Since we are creatures of habit, we have specific *japa* habits. Improving *japa* entails creating new and improved *japa* habits, thus making good *japa* your norm.

This week, work on overcoming some bad *japa* habits by developing some new and better habits.

Write down the realizations you get by doing this.

You can also share your realizations and read other devotees' realizations on our app.

Just scan this QR code.

Note that all realizations will not necessarily be positive. Sometimes, you might simply realize how difficult it is to change. These kinds of realizations make you aware that you will have to work harder at improving than you might have thought. Therefore, even the "bad" becomes an inspiration to improve.

CHAPTER 2

The Importance of Japa in the Practice of Bhakti

Is There Anything More Important Than Chanting?

Chanting is the most powerful way to become Kṛṣṇa conscious. The following statements explain the importance of *japa* in *bhakti*.

"Of all the regulative principles,the spiritual master's order to chant 16 rounds is most essential." (*Śrī Caitanya-caritāmṛta*, *Madhya-līlā* 22.113, Purport)

In initiation letters, it was common for Śrīla Prabhupāda to write that chanting sixteen rounds is your ticket back to Godhead. After chanting on Giriraj Swami's beads, Prabhupāda wrote him saying, "Your beads are your link to Kṛṣṇa."

Prabhupāda once told Trivikrama Mahārāja, "This chanting is the essence of our philosophy."

Obviously, you can't minimize the essence of our philosophy, your link to Kṛṣṇa, and the most essential instruction of the spiritual master without it having a negative effect on your spiritual life. Conversely, you can't maximize the importance you give your *japa* without it having a tremendously positive effect on your Kṛṣṇa consciousness.

The quality of our chanting tends to improve in proportion to the priority we give to *japa* in our lives.

This week, as you chant your rounds, meditate on the primary importance of chanting the holy names in the practice of *japa* and allow this meditation to help you become more enthused and absorbed in chanting.

Write down the realizations you get this week by applying this principle to your *japa*.

You can also share your realizations and read other devotees' realizations on my app.

Just scan this QR code.

scan me

CHAPTER 3

Your Japa Blueprint

What's Your Blueprint?

We all have a *japa* blueprint. This blueprint manifests in the quality of our chanting, which tends to be more or less the same every day. This works for us or against us, depending on the quality of the blueprint.

Chanting good *japa* consistently is possible for you. It's a matter of making excellent *japa* normal. As poor or average *japa* tends to be a habit that is repeated daily, good or excellent *japa* also can easily become a habit.

However, it does require work to change your blueprint. The key is to be steady with your improvements. The latest science tells us that it takes 66 days of consistent behavior to develop a new habit. So, for the next two months or so, if you maintain improvements to your chanting, like putting out more effort, focusing more, or not thinking about your day when you chant, you will then have developed some good *japa* habits that will hopefully remain with you for the rest of your life.

You can start to improve your *japa* blueprint by bringing more awareness to your current level of chanting. Notice what you habitually do that is either helpful or harmful to your *japa*. Then, improve upon what is already working for you, eliminate what is not working, and add practices and attitudes that help.

As your *japa* improves, you will see positive changes in your Kṛṣṇa consciousness. Change your *japa*, change your life.

There are also subconscious habitual thoughts that affect our chanting. One subconscious mantra that many of us chant when we begin our *japa* is, "Oh no, 16 rounds," as we dread the austerity of having to control our minds for two hours. Another similar subconscious mantra that tends to flow through our *japa* is (sometimes it is not so subconscious), "When is this going to be over?" We need to eliminate these and other similar mantras from our habitual subconscious thinking.

As you chant this week, become aware of the other "mantras" going on in your head that may be undermining quality *japa* and replace them with more positive expressions that reflect appreciation of the holy names.

Write down the realizations you get this week by applying these practices to your *japa*.

You can also share your realizations and read other devotees' realizations on my app.

Just scan this QR code.

scan me

CHAPTER 4

How Physiology Affects the Mind

Sit Properly

Several times Śrīla Prabhupāda interrupted a lecture or a *japa* session to tell someone to "Sit properly." In the purport to *Śrīmad-Bhāgavatam* 3.28.5, Prabhupāda writes: "First one must be able to sit properly, and then the mind and attention will become steady enough for practicing yoga."

How we sit, stand, or walk, or whether our eyes wander when chanting, affects our ability to concentrate and pray. Generally, the more your body moves around, or the more you look around while chanting, the more your mind will be distracted.

Remember, *japa* is meditation. The goal is to be absorbed in thinking of Kṛṣṇa. Slouching over, sight-seeing while taking a *japa* walk, looking around while sitting in one place, etc. will all affect your ability to concentrate.

Chanting is best done in the mode of goodness. I recommend that at least some of your rounds should be chanted sitting down, with your eyes focused or closed, and your rounds chanted softly. You will find that by doing this, the mind will tend to be calmer. If you get antsy too quickly when you sit in one place, it is probably a sign that you need more *sattva* in your life – and especially more *sattva* in your chanting.

The reverse is also true. When you focus, when you pray while chanting, and when you are making an effort to be absorbed in the name, you will tend to automatically have the posture mentioned above. So when your eyes are wandering and your body slouching or moving around a lot, become aware that you may be doing this as a result of already being distracted or disturbed. You can also try chanting some rounds with your bead-bag over your heart as this may bring you into a more prayerful mood.

Write down the realizations you get this week by applying these practices to your *japa*.

You can also share your realizations and read other devotees' realizations on my app.

Just scan this QR code.

CHAPTER 5

Be Present

Be Here Now

Doing one thing while thinking of something else is to not "be present." It's a symptom of the mode of passion and ignorance. As mentioned in the last installment, in order to focus on hearing the mantra well, you want to at least be in the mode of goodness while chanting.

In goodness, passions are quieted. Hankering and lamentation are subdued.

To be present during *japa* requires that you be absent from the things in your life that don't support your *japa*. It's common while chanting to think about what happened yesterday, what will happen later today, or what is bothering you, and thus not "be present" to your *japa*.

To really "be present" requires that you leave your ordinary world aside while doing *japa*. Think of chanting as entering Kṛṣṇa's world, and putting your world on hold. I like to visualize leaving my house (my life) and going into my *japa-kutir* (Kṛṣṇa's world).

A big mistake commonly made is to focus on the number of rounds you have chanted and on how many rounds you have left. The goal is not to chant 16 rounds, the goal is to chant quality *japa*. Of course, I am not saying that you don't have to chant 16 rounds, but if you believe that you are successful simply by the fact that you have completed your quota, not because you have chanted well, you have made your *japa* into a ritual. And *bhakti* is the antithesis of ritual.

When we are chanting the mantra, "When is this going to be over?" underneath our *japa*, we are really saying, "Kṛṣṇa, I find it unpleasant being with You." This is the real reason we are not present to our *japa*. The mind wants to think about everything under the sun other than the holy name. We have been competing with Kṛṣṇa for so long, it can be difficult to sit with Him for a few hours and relish His association in His name.

Prabhupāda said that Kṛṣṇa is in His name. We should be meditating on this while chanting. We can't intellectually understand this, but we at least must treat the holy name as Kṛṣṇa. It is just like Deity worship. We may not fully understand or appreciate how Kṛṣṇa is in the Deity, but we treat the Deity as Kṛṣṇa. By treating the Deity as Kṛṣṇa, we come to realize His presence in this form and we become more and more attached to the Deity. In the same way, if we treat the holy name as Kṛṣṇa, we come to realize more and more how He is present in His name. As we realize His presence in His name, we naturally become more present when chanting.

In other words, lack of presence while chanting reflects a lack of realization of His presence in His name. But the only way to get this realization is to constantly remind ourselves that Kṛṣṇa is kindly appearing to us in His names, and thus appreciate the wonderful opportunity we have to so easily get His association.

Write down the realizations you get this week by trying to be more present to your *japa*. Also, let me know what how this helps you get closer to the holy names.

Just scan this QR code to share your realizations.

scan me

CHAPTER 6

Sacred Space

Creating a Sacred Place for a Sacred Relationship

If you were studying for an important and difficult exam, and you had the choice of studying in a library or at a party, which would you choose? Since the right environment is conducive to good study, you'd choose the library. Similarly, the environment in which you chant affects the quality of your *japa*. Therefore, it's essential that you create a "Sacred Space" for your *japa*.

A Sacred Space is an environment that fully supports your *japa*. It should be a place in which nothing else but *japa* is going on, and a place that fosters concentration on and absorption in the holy names.

A Sacred Space not only includes where you chant, but also when you chant. A Sacred Space is both a place and a time that are most conducive to good *japa*.

As we all know, early in the morning is the best time to chant. So one of the most important *sādhana* practices you can do to improve your rounds is rise early.

Also, you will notice that daily chanting in the same place and at the same time empowers that space; it becomes the place where good rounds are chanted.

A Sacred Space can also be created wherever you are. Let's say you are at the temple and some devotees are talking during *japa*, or for example, on festival days, a lot of things are going on in the temple room during *japa* time.

As strange as it may sound, you will need to find a Sacred Space at the temple, a place away from the commotion where you can chant without being disturbed and where you can concentrate.

The same holds true when you travel. If you must chant on a bus, airplane, or train, do your best to zone out the rest of the world so you can focus on your chanting. You will need to make a little Sacred Space *japa* bubble when you are out in public.

I have found that when chanting in these kinds of crowded areas, I can often create a Sacred Space when I focus on feeling the vibration of the mantra. When I feel the holy name vibrating in my body, it tends to pull my attention away from external sounds and sights and naturally internally focuses my mind. (You can also try this when you are at home.)

Chanting is a sacred time for developing our sacred relationship. Kṛṣṇa certainly deserves our full attention. Making a Sacred Space for chanting is like setting up a nice dinner table for a loved one. Although we can eat dinner anywhere, it is more special with a beautiful tablecloth, low lighting, flowers, candlelight, and nice background music. Our Sacred Space is meant to be a special place where we can most readily and deeply connect with Kṛṣṇa.

Ultimately the real Sacred Space is meant to be within us. But the external environment affects the internal environment.

Write down the realizations you get this week by creating your Sacred Space. I'd like to hear how you are doing, and what challenges you face, so please share your realizations.

Just scan this QR code to share your realizations.

scan me

CHAPTER 7

Entering Into the Mood and Meaning of the Mantra

It All Depends on Feeling

The *mahā-mantra* is a prayer in which the devotee petitions the Lord for pure love. Prabhupāda said that the quality of one's chanting depends on feeling, or the intensity of one's prayer.

Feeling is first expressed in the heart before it's expressed in words. The same is true with chanting. Kṛṣṇa is moved by love, not by parrot-like repetition. Our challenge is not just to get our rounds done, it is to bring devotional meditation into our chanting. Śrīla Bhaktisiddhānta Sarasvatī said, "The holy name is not lip deep, it's heart deep."

Chanting is like the genuine cry of a child for its mother. The *mahā-mantra* has many meanings. Here is a list of some of them:

"Please engage me in your service,"

"Oh my friend, Oh my friend,"

"Please accept me,"

"Please pull my heart to you."

And there are many other meanings to the mantra that have been given to us by the previous *ācāryas*.

The mood of your chanting is expressed through the particular meaning of the mantra you are meditating upon. As you chant, enter more deeply into the meaning and intent of the *mahā-mantra*. You may meditate on one of the meanings the *ācāryas* have given, what it means to you, or a prayer to overcome a difficult *anartha* or situation you are dealing with. Or you may pray to the holy name simply for pure devotional service.

This kind of meditative chanting prevents what I call "Courtesy *Japa*." Courtesy *japa* is done as an obligation to a particular number of rounds we have vowed to chant, a courtesy to that number. Courtesy *japa* tends to be monotonous, robotic, and mechanical.

In contrast to this, chanting is all about feeling, both expressing your feelings and prayers to Kṛṣṇa and also feeling Kṛṣṇa's presence in His holy names. (Prabhupāda said that you can feel Kṛṣṇa in His name).

Devotees often ask how to control the mind during *japa*. I find that if I feelingly pray to the holy names, if I express my heart to Kṛṣṇa through His names, I transcend the fluctuations of my mind. In other words, when the heart expresses itself, the mind tends to turn off – or just follows the call of the heart. But when the mind is active and distracted, our heart tends to close. So the solution to controlling the mind is to open the heart.

As you chant, reflect on what you are trying to achieve by chanting. This is what I call "intentional chanting." Why are you chanting? Is it just to finish your quota, or is it to come closer to Kṛṣṇa through pure devotional service? As you reflect on what the *mahā-mantra* means, and how that meaning relates to you personally, you naturally enter deeper into your chanting.

Write down the realizations you get this week by meditating on the meaning of the mantra.

Just scan this QR code to share your realizations.

scan me

CHAPTER 8

Chanting Is a Relationship

Chanting Is Not Just a Process; It's a Relationship.

Chanting is one of the nine processes of *bhakti*, but we can easily define or relate it to a process as something mechanical and think that externally executing the process will guarantee specific results.

When you think of chanting as a relationship, you become aware that the relationship is suffering when you don't chant well (which is why you suffer). Since Kṛṣṇa wants an intimate relationship with you, and since He wants you to come back to Him, He is also unhappy when you don't chant well and happy when you do chant well.

We are told that Kṛṣṇa has everything. Yet, there is one thing He doesn't have – our heart. And this is what He wants most. Chanting is a way to give back to Kṛṣṇa what He wants most, a relationship with us.

I like to see the *mahā-mantra* as a gift of love. Kṛṣṇa is offering us a relationship with Him through the chanting of His holy names. The *mahā-mantra* is the personification of Kṛṣṇa's love for us, and the love for Himself that we develop through chanting the mantra. The *mahā-mantra* is like the fishing line of love that Kṛṣṇa extends to all of us. How fortunate we are. And how unfortunate we can be to take the holy names for granted, to mumble off our "snick, snicks, Ram, Rams" while our minds travel the universe.

Allow yourself to feel Kṛṣṇa's affection for you while you chant. Feel how much He wants a relationship with you. If He didn't care about you and me, He wouldn't have incarnated as Caitanya

Mahāprabhu, neither would He have sent Śrīla Prabhupāda to deliver the world. As you allow yourself to feel Kṛṣṇa's affection, appreciate your great fortune in being able to chant the holy names and reciprocate with His loving call and the loving embrace of Rādhā and Kṛṣṇa.

A process, as opposed to a relationship, is done without consciousness. A process alone doesn't express affection; you must express affection yourself. You can offer a gift to someone in order to get their favor, but it won't communicate affection if offered with ulterior motive. Even though you did what appears to be a kind or proper act, the act is only meant to be a medium to express your love. An act alone doesn't necessarily express affection. Similarly, the *mahā-mantra* is the medium through which we express our devotion, sincerity, and pure motivation to Kṛṣṇa. Chanting alone is not necessarily an expression of devotion.

For example, what is the difference between an ordinary person's cooking and Mother Yaśodā's cooking? They both cut vegetables, use a pot, and cook on fire. The difference is the consciousness. Similarly, what is the difference between two people who externally perfectly execute the process of chanting (sitting straight, pronouncing properly, eyes focused, etc.)? The difference is in the consciousness. Two people are chanting what appears to be the same mantra, but may in actuality be chanting two different mantras. One may be chanting for material benefits or liberation, while the other is chanting for pure devotional service.

Pure devotional service is defined as service done without motivation for material gain or liberation. Similarly, pure chanting is chanting done with the motivation only to please Kṛṣṇa. Can we chant purely if we are not pure? Yes. Just chant with the motivation to become a pure devotee and to please Kṛṣṇa with your chanting.

Sometimes you may wish to chant with the meditation that you are chanting just to please Kṛṣṇa. As you chant, your only thought and your only motive should be to please Kṛṣṇa by your chanting. This is the meaning of "pure chanting."

Write down the realizations you get this week by chanting in the mood of chanting is a relationship.

Just scan this QR code to share your realizations.

scan me

CHAPTER 9

Aligning Your Life With the Holy Names

Everything You Do Affects You

Good *japa* does not exist in a vacuum. What you do in the day is reflected in your *japa*. A more Kṛṣṇa conscious lifestyle naturally lends itself to better *japa*. So the more important *japa* is in your life, the more concerned you will become about doing things throughout the day that will nourish your chanting. If you allow yourself to do things that undermine the quality of your *japa*, it is likely a sign that you are not giving your *japa* the attention or priority it requires.

Be more conscious of how your daily activities affect your *japa*. For example, before you decide to stay up late at night, minimize your *sādhana* to get a project done, or take on more service, or a new and more demanding job, reflect on how these decisions will affect your rounds.

Another common lifestyle obstacle to good *japa* is not rising early. If this is a challenge for you, organizing your life in a way that you can rise early will prove to be one of the best things you can do to improve your *japa*.

Living our lives in a way that fosters good rounds is a science. If you allow your life to be predominated by the modes of passion and ignorance, your mind will tend to be more disturbed and distracted when you chant. You will be competing with the passion and ignorance of the previous day in your attempt to focus. (Can you relate to this?) When this happens, it can take many rounds to clear those modes away. Thus, it may take you eight rounds just to calm your mind down enough to hear your rounds. Ideally, we should be hearing our rounds well from the very first bead.

This is most desirable. And it is possible.

Many devotees relate how reading the pastimes of the Lord helps their *japa* because they naturally think of the Lord's pastimes while chanting. One devotee tells how his *japa* is always good when he has introduced people to the *mahā-mantra* the day before. Other devotees relate how their *japa* is always more relishable after an especially ecstatic day of devotional service (brought about by overcoming a difficult situation, accomplishing something special, doing more austerities than usual, etc.).

The reality is that everything we do, see, speak, and hear affects our consciousness and thus will subtly or grossly support or undermine our *japa*. Applying techniques to improve our *japa* is important; but it is not the entire equation. What we do in the other 22 hours of our day influences us, and thus our chanting, to one degree or another.

List some activities that you feel are detrimental to your *japa* and what you might do to overcome them. Also, list some things you can do during your day that would positively impact your *japa*.

You can read more about this topic in *Volume 1* of this book (Section Two, Chapter 12: Living the Holy Name Lifestyle).

CHAPTER 10

Bringing It Home

What can you do to ensure that you take advantage of these lessons as well as continue to improve your *japa*?

Improving *japa* is an ongoing process. Utilizing the tools in this course (and the many other tools offered in *The Japa Workshop*) is meant to continue throughout your life. If you do this, you will gradually realize dimensions to the holy name you never knew existed.

Many devotees believe that if they focus on improving their rounds, and make good *japa* a priority, they can improve their *japa* to the point that they can consistently chant good rounds. They are right.

There are, however, other devotees who doubt they can consistently chant good rounds. These devotees don't make much effort to follow the principles and practices outlined in this course. They don't believe that they can actually improve their *japa* that much.

Why?

They fear that their bad *japa* habits are so deeply engrained that any attempt to improve or change will only be temporary. Again they will fall back into their old habits. The problem with devotees who think this way is that they are also right! No one is going to improve much if they maintain these kinds of fears.

If we focus on what we don't want, what we are afraid might happen, then this is what tends to happen. On the contrary, if we focus on our goals, on what we would like to achieve, that is what tends to happen.

What kind of *japa* would you like to achieve? If you had a wish fulfilling tree that could offer you whatever kind of *japa* you wanted (in terms of quality and experience), what would it look like? This is what you should meditate on and pray for rather than focus on how bad you think your *japa* will remain.

Even though you may have chanted poorly for years, you can change this by following the guidelines in these courses (and the other workshops I give) and, most importantly, by being determined to improve.

With this kind of determination and effort, Kṛṣṇa will give you a special taste for the holy name. Kṛṣṇa responds to your efforts. It is by your effort that you attract His mercy, and it is by His mercy that you advance.

SECTION FIVE

How to Make a Marriage Work

CHAPTER 1

Why Marriages Don't Last

This chapter is inspired by the many letters that I've received asking how to choose a partner and why marriages don't last; it is my attempt to take all of my responses to these letters and organize them into something cohesive.

I feel it important to share this information because stable marriages are becoming more and more of a challenge today, and I want to do my part in helping devotees make their marriages successful. I hope that the following will be useful either to you or to someone you know.

Choosing the Right Partner

One of the most important elements in creating a lasting marriage is choosing the right partner.

Having a compatibility chart and/or doing pre-marital counseling is advisable, but in addition to this it is important to be with the person you are considering marrying (or engaged to) over a one- or two- year period before marriage, and also to be with them in a large number of situations. This helps you to get to know what the person is really like. If you don't do this, you may only get to know the person well after marriage, and you might find out things about him or her that surprise you, which having known before may have caused you to reconsider marrying them – or even convinced you not to marry them.

Personal Issues

For example, sometimes you find that people have serious emotional issues that makes it difficult for them to open up, to be reasonable in some situations, to trust you, or to get close to you. Sometimes they become easily (possibly also seriously) depressed when going through difficulties. Or they need to be right, have their way, are terribly irresponsible or immature, can't listen to anyone, or can't compromise.

These personal problems make it difficult for them to be good partners. They would need to work on these issues before marriage. If they don't, these issues could be the cause of a very unhappy or miserable relationship.

Abusive Men

Additionally, there are many anger, abuse, and violence issues that are becoming more and more common today among men, and if a man has these tendencies, the longer you are together before marriage, the more likely it will be for you to see warning signs of a potentially abusive relationship.

One way to prevent marrying a potentially abusive man is to do some background check on him.

Does he have a history of anger issues, violence with women – or men – etc.? It is not uncommon for men to lie about former failed relationships, either covering them up or blaming the failure on their former partner. So be aware of this. No woman can cause a man to be physically violent; it is his personal problem.

Also, if he blames his relationship failure(s) on his former partner(s), this is a red flag. It means if the relationship with you starts to fail, he will blame it on you. In fact, it is likely he will blame all marital problems on you.

Hiding Defects

Here's another problem to be aware of: Because a person wants to marry, often they will do their best to hide their defects (you may do this as well). And because you like this person very much and you feel happy being with them, even though you notice defects that would normally be of concern, you don't pay much attention to them (or you are simply oblivious of them). The euphoria of "love" is like a drug which can even make you think their faults are "cute." But later on many of those faults will no longer be seen as "cute," and some of them can become the cause of serious problems in the marriage.

I Don't Like You

Linked to not knowing each other well enough before marriage is another common problem: after living together for some time, the couple realizes they don't really like one another that much. So how did they end up together in the first place if in fact they really had little in common? Because physical attraction dominated. Their external attraction brought them together and made them think they loved one another and were a great match. It is when the physical attraction starts to wane that some couples realize what they didn't realize before: they don't really like one another much.

A very Kṛṣṇa conscious couple could deal with this by making their spiritual advancement the center of their relationship and being more tolerant of their differences. They could still be quite happy in their Kṛṣṇa consciousness. They would accept that their marriage *karma* is not great but still being dutiful they would live together peacefully.

Still, even Prabhupāda admits that if a match is not compatible, the couple will not be very happy together.

Do Compatibility Charts Work?

But you might ask, "If they did a compatibility chart and/or premarital counseling, how is it that later on they find they don't like being together? Sometimes even couples with compatible charts end up getting divorced. There is more to making a marriage work than having a compatible chart. And this is why it is recommended to get to know someone well before deciding to marry them.

Men Are From Mars, Women From Venus

Another reason marriage may not last is because those entering marriage know little about marriage and the opposite sex. When they enter the marriage arena they don't know how to play by the rules because they don't know the rules. It's common that people have little idea what it takes to make a marriage work well and what are all the differences between men and women.

Unhealthy Paradigms

A big cause of short-lived marriages is unhealthy marriage paradigms, some of which may be picked up in ISKCON. These include negative connotations about marriage, the opposite sex, etc. In the name of helping one progress on the spiritual path, some of our preaching may undermine values necessary for a healthy marriage. If one enters a marriage with negative connotations, it can be difficult to make the marriage work well. (Note: This is usually a problem with men.)

Cheating

A common cause of divorce these days is that one of the spouses becomes attracted to another person. This means that they don't view their marriage as a sacred duty. Rather, if they don't get enjoyment from their spouse, they look for it elsewhere. This can make it impossible for their marriage to continue, even if the culprit spouse apologizes and is remorseful. This is because the cheated spouse may not be able to forgive, and without forgiveness they normally find it unbearable to continue the relationship. Or if the relationship continues, it becomes cold, distant, and full of mistrust.

No Money

Financial problems can cause divorce. The husband doesn't provide well because he is not well-educated and can't find a good job. Or maybe he cannot keep a job, or is just lazy and doesn't want to work much. Or he has a low-paying job and needs to work two jobs to make ends meet and hardly has time for his family.

It also happens that one or both of the spouses overspend and put the family in debt. Or one of them regularly makes big purchases without consulting the other.

I Lost Interest in Kṛṣṇa consciousness

There is another situation: one of the partners loses interest in Kṛṣṇa consciousness and the couple starts drifting apart. They don't necessarily have to drift apart, but the more Kṛṣṇa conscious partner may get upset or discouraged by the lessened interest of their partner. Or the less Kṛṣṇa conscious partner may want to limit the devotional activities of his or her spouse.

There is another scenario, slightly different but in the same vein: both spouses are good devotees but one of the spouses becomes detached from *gṛhastha-āśrama*, showing very little interest in family life although the couple is not at the *vānaprastha* stage of life. They neglect their families because of their service, seeing service as important and family as an impediment to their Kṛṣṇa consciousness. In this sense, Kṛṣṇa consciousness, when not applied in a healthy and balanced way, becomes the cause of divorce.

Values Change As We Age

Then there are situations in which values differ significantly. One wants to live in a hut on a farm and grow food and the other wants to live in a high-rise apartment in a big city. One wants to spend their life in service to Kṛṣṇa and the other wants both to work at high-paying jobs. One wants two kids and the other wants none, or one wants a lot of kids and the other only one.

You might say that if they did pre-marital counseling they could have avoided this problem. But this is not always the case, because sometimes people's values change later in life. For example, at the age of 22 one may say they don't want any children, but at the age of 28 they may desire to have many.

So if you marry, you will need to be flexible. Don't be surprised if your spouse who wanted to live on a farm in a small cob home when he/she was 22 may find that lifestyle unappealing when he/she is 35 and now wants a nice home in suburbia with all modern amenities.

Not Fit for Marriage

Sometimes a couple marries to realize after some time that they don't like being married (they realize they were not ready yet for marriage or that they are just not cut out for marriage). The marriage naturally degrades as they have difficulty being married and don't have the strength or grounding to be a dutiful spouse anyway. If you feel you want to be married, make sure you are really ready for it, and make sure your potential partner is ready as well.

Background Check

Learn more about your partner's history. Does he/she have a history of failed relationships – not just with the opposite sex, but in temples, work, with parents, siblings, etc.? It is rare that partners do this, yet it is common to later find out, after a failed relationship, that this person had a history of similarly failed relationships.

Addictions

There is also the situation in which one of the spouses becomes helplessly fallen by becoming addicted to drugs, alcohol, sex, etc., and life at home becomes unhealthy for the kids, the spouse, or both.

Not Mentally Stable

You might come to find out, as does sometimes happen, that your spouse is actually not mentally stable – perhaps even clinically mentally ill and they never told you. It could also happen that it is during the course of the marriage that the mental illness develops. The problem is often that they need to take medications to be stable, but they don't, or they sometimes forget, and living with them may become impossible. Or sometimes, the medications don't help that much, and it requires extreme patience and tolerance to deal with them – more tolerance than you can muster on a consistent basis. Again, learning more about the person's history could reveal these mental problems. I am not saying that knowing this reality would necessarily deter you from marrying them, but at least you would be aware of the potential challenges you will inevitably face with them.

Health Care

What if your spouse becomes crippled or seriously ill and your whole life revolves around caring for them and you hit a point in which you have a breakdown, can't continue to do it, or find it difficult to be around them all the time?

When you marry, you take responsibility for your spouse in "happiness or distress."

Gay Marriage

Or maybe you find out your partner is a homosexual (and may even be having homosexual relations). Again, better try to find out as much as possible about your potential spouse before you marry.

Why Did We Marry?

There are many other causes of divorce, most of which center around having a misunderstanding of the purpose of marriage (enjoyment versus service, control versus support, etc.). Devotees may enter marriage with expectations of happiness based on material conceptions that are both unrealistic and not Kṛṣṇa conscious. Marriage is for spiritual advancement, and happiness in a Kṛṣṇa conscious marriage is a by-product of the spouses effectively helping one another advance. As such, if enjoyment and the happiness derived from it is their main reason to be married and they cannot find such fulfillment in their marriage, they may want to get out of it in search of happiness in another relationship.

External Pressure to Marry

Yet another cause of divorce is external pressure to get married in the first place. Sometimes a devotee may receive strong recommendations from a senior devotee, relative, or authority to get married to a particular person whom the devotee barely knows, or has not had enough time to associate with. The marriage takes place and both partners soon realize they are not compatible with each other or were not actually ready for marriage.

Internal Pressure to Marry

There may also be an internal pressure to marry. One may be hitting an age where if they don't marry soon, then they won't be able to have children or it will be difficult to find an eligible partner. Sometimes one wants to marry so badly that they are not honest about themselves – they hide some major fault or something dark about their past in order to appear more appealing to potential partners. The parents of a potential spouse may also hide information about their son or daughter, knowing that if you became aware of it then you wouldn't marry them.

Third Party Interference

A similar cause for divorce is interference from third parties. Such interference can seem benevolent. For example, one partner may feel a lot of respect for a senior authority who is giving him/her advice on such things as marriage, professional life, raising children, service, etc. However, the other spouse may find such advice unacceptable or disconnected from the reality of the couple's particular situation. So be careful about making decisions recommended by third parties that are upsetting to your partner (gurus understanding this reality will be careful about giving advice that would be upsetting to a disciple's spouse).

What's Most Important?

Now having said all of the above, I believe the most fundamental problem causing a bad marriage is that men are not being men and women are not being women. Many men don't fully understand what it means to be a man. This means that they don't understand women well, and thus they don't support them well, they don't respect them well, and they don't tolerate their frailties well. And women are never happy living with such so-called men!

And when women act like men – controlling the man, not respecting him, or not supporting him – he will find the situation extremely frustrating, or even unbearable.

Another foundational reason for divorce is that the couple never really committed deeply enough in the first place to make the marriage work. Because they see divorce as a solution to their problems, they think they can always run out the back door rather than thinking, "Divorce is not an option, and we have to make this work." In the West, we are not trained to see marriage as a lifetime commitment. Rather, we are trained to think, "If it doesn't work out, try again." The joke is that on the wedding day the relatives say, "She will make a good first wife for him!"

The Man's Responsibility

Prabhupāda said divorce is usually due to a woman's weakness. But when a woman has a good husband, Prabhupāda says she will be happy and in *sattva-guṇa*. Therefore, if the man makes her happy and helps her to be Kṛṣṇa conscious, it is less likely that she will leave him. Of course, I am sure that there are some women whose husbands can never make them happy no matter how hard the husbands try, but generally if the husband treats his wife well and is a good example of Kṛṣṇa consciousness, the wife will be satisfied.

Should I Marry?

Now, maybe after reading this you have become very concerned about entering marriage. Well, you should be; because if you are not, you might end up as part of the divorce statistics. If you are going to marry, be aware that aside from the benefits you will receive there will be many new challenges, and it is not going to always be easy. All your problems will not go away when you marry, and some new ones will visit you. But as long as you are aware of this, you are better situated to deal with the realities of marriage, make it work, and be an example of an ideal Kṛṣṇa conscious couple.

As it is said, "Marriage is not a destination; it is a journey."

In Conclusion

Understand that in the beginning of a relationship you will not know enough about the person to conclude whether they are the right match for you. Maybe you sense that they are, but that sense needs to be confirmed by getting to know one another well. And it also needs to be backed up by understanding as much as you can about the nature of the opposite sex and the nature of the *gṛhastha-āśrama*.

Read about and listen to workshops on marriage; talk to experienced devotees about marriage. The more you know about this *āśrama* before you enter it, the better. (One potential resource is my website, www.mahatmadas.com, where there are thirty lectures on the *gṛhastha-āśrama* that I feel will be extremely helpful for you if you are exploring this topic.)

Is There More?

There are other reasons for divorce, and the above is not meant to be an exhaustive list. This chapter is meant to help you learn more about the potential pitfalls of marriage, knowing which can help you make more intelligent choices about who might be the best marriage partner for you.

"An ounce of prevention is worth a pound of cure."

CHAPTER 2

Husband As Guru

An unmarried female devotee once shared with me that a man was interested in getting to know her, and that in their discussions he had mentioned, "the husband is the guru". She asked me for guidance on the subject.

The following is what I wrote to clarify for her (and him) what it means for a husband to be a guru and what it doesn't mean, for misunderstanding what this means will be the cause of an unhappy marriage. I expect that some men will not agree with what I share below (although I doubt that any women will disagree), and for this reason I had some reservations about making this response public. I have nevertheless decided to share it, because it is an important discussion that deserves to be addressed.

Is It the Woman's Fault?

Prabhupāda writes that a failed marriage is usually the woman's fault, and that if a woman has a good husband, she will stay loyal. That said, I often tell men, "Don't make it difficult for your spouse to be a good wife."

The husband as the guru of the wife is an interesting concept. Some men operate under the paradigm that, "since I am the guru of my wife, she is duty-bound to do anything I ask of her." I am not saying that it isn't the duty of the wife to submissively serve the husband. However, the idea that a husband has the right to be over-demanding of his wife reflects a misunderstanding of the duty of the husband.

You might think, "Are there really many men in ISKCON today who are that demanding?" The answer is yes. And not only are there demanding men in ISKCON, some (perhaps many) of them are even more demanding of their wives than men outside of ISKCON. My experience is that many men have misunderstood Prabhupāda's statements about the duty of a husband and the duty of a wife.

We have a higher divorce rate in ISKCON than in the outside society. We also have a high rate of unhappy marriages (devotees who remain married because they are dutiful, not because they are happily married). This problem is commonly caused by male devotees misunderstanding what it means to be a man.

Exercise

1. What is your understanding of your duties to your spouse as defined by Śrīla Prabhupāda and successful *gṛhasthas*?
2. On a scale of 1 to 10, how well are you following these duties?
3. What are some things you can do to be a better spouse?

Arrogance

In *śāstra* we read that the husband is the guru. Many men believe this means the wife should obediently do whatever is asked of her, no matter how difficult or unreasonable it may be. But the husband does not have the right to be unreasonably demanding. This is not the kind of relationship a guru and disciple have.

When Prabhupāda was asked by his disciple Visala Das, "Should the wife do whatever the husband says?" Prabhupāda replied, "And you should be so arrogant?" (*Following Śrīla Prabhupada –* Remembrances by Yadubara Dasa)

What does it mean to be a guru to a wife and what does it mean for the wife to see her husband as a guru? Guru is one who is moving towards Kṛṣṇa. If the husband is moving towards Kṛṣṇa, naturally the wife will follow. And even if she doesn't follow him perfectly, by serving him she partakes in his spiritual advancement. So husbands, your main duty as guru of your wives is to be steadily advancing in Kṛṣṇa consciousness.

Exercise

Considering that "guru is one who is moving towards Kṛṣṇa," what are some things you can do to make your marriage more Krsna conscious?

A Guru Shows Affection

A guru does not push the disciple beyond his or her limits. Neither should a husband. A guru encourages the disciple according to their propensity so that they are enlivened and happy. Women married to overly demanding men are rarely happy. This is because a woman wants a husband who is affectionate, not dictatorial.

Of course, a guru guides the disciple. But to guide the wife, and for the wife to want to listen to the husband, she must be well taken care of emotionally, not just taken care of materially. Disciples follow their guru because of the love and care they receive from him. The guru is full of affection for his disciple, always giving to the disciple more than the disciple is giving back. Thus, the disciple wants to reciprocate. The same dynamic should be there with a husband.

Walk Your Talk

The husband/wife relationship is not meant to mimic a formal guru/disciple relationship, because the guru/disciple relationship is predominated by awe and reverence, whereas the husband/wife relationship is predominated by friendship and conjugal affection. Thus, "husband as guru" refers primarily to the man being spiritually strong, setting a good example, showing affection, and inspiring his wife in spiritual life by his example.

Being guru means to "walk your talk." If a man does this, then naturally the woman will respect him. If he wants respect, he must act in a way that commands respect. If he doesn't act respectfully, but only demands respect, he should not be surprised – or upset – when he doesn't receive the respect he demands.

Exercise

1. On a scale of 1-10, how well do you walk your talk? What do you think can help you do this better?
2. What do you think receiving respect entails? On a scale of 1-10, to what extent do you show the respect that you expect or hope to receive from your spouse and others?

Listen to Me

If the husband is guru, doesn't that mean that it's his duty to instruct his wife? In Vedic times women did not receive *dīkṣā*; thus, because the husband had been trained up in executing spiritual life in the *gurukula*, he would take up the responsibility of passing on to his wife the knowledge he had received from his guru. Today, women have access to instructions from many gurus and teachers, and so the role of the husband as her sole spiritual teacher has changed.

Women appreciate husbands who follow Kṛṣṇa consciousness well; that said, as mentioned above, it is unlikely that he is the person from whom she receives most of her spiritual instructions from. This is because the husband/wife relationship is not primarily a teacher/student relationship; it is a partnership. Still, if a couple has a good relationship and the husband is a good devotee, the wife will appreciate the husband sharing Kṛṣṇa consciousness with her.

And men: beware that sometimes in the name of doing your duty to instruct your wife, you latch into a fault-finding session. And then you scratch your head, wondering why your wife is reluctant to listen to you in the future. When instructing your wife, especially in sensitive areas, do it with care, affection, and sensitivity. If in the name of instructing your wife you end up making her upset, unhappy, or discouraged, then you are failing in your duty as a husband/guru.

Exercise

Give examples of how you tried to help your wife and it ended up disturbing her. How could you have done it better?

You Are Always a Servant

Men: remember that you are a servant, not a master. It is sometimes a challenge to remember this in household life, but it is written on just about every page of Śrīla Prabhupāda's books, and I have yet to read any disclaimer stating that being a servant doesn't apply to your role as a husband.

Did I hear someone say, "If I do this then I will be controlled by my wife, and I won't be a real man!"?

Be a Real Man

Being masculine doesn't mean controlling the wife to ensure that one is not controlled by her. To be masculine means to make one's wife happy, fulfill her needs, and be sensitive to her ups and downs. If a man does not do this, then he is not acting like a real man. Rather, it means that he is being controlled by the lower modes of nature and is being more feminine than masculine.

When *śāstra* speaks of being controlled by women, it is not what most men think. To patiently take care of a woman's needs, to listen to her when she is upset, to be a stable force for her when she is overly emotional, is what it means to be a man. If a man can do this, he is sense-controlled. If he can't do this, he is being controlled by a woman's behavior. This is what it really means to be controlled by a woman.

Unfortunately, many men are not good at being tolerant with their wives, and react to difficult situations by telling their wives they are emotional and they should just pull themselves together. Sometimes when the wife is upset, they will argue or fight with her rather than try to understand and help her. Despite what some men think, fighting with a woman has nothing to do with being a strong man. It is the sign of a man who succumbs to the modes of passion and ignorance. Somehow, this fact is so clear to women yet so unclear to men.

Kṛṣṇa is the supreme male – the supreme masculine – and He is submissive to Rādhārāṇī. Kṛṣṇa is never rough and tough with Rādhārāṇī. He doesn't yell at Her or try to control Her. He just tries to make Her happy. This is what it means to be a male. Of course, the movies portray males as being rough and tough, beating up other big rough and tough guys. But factually those "macho" men are only impressing other men, not other women. Women don't like these "tough" guys. They like men who are sensitive to their needs.

Men who don't want to (or can't) regularly serve the needs of a woman as described above should not marry. If they already are married, they should understand that it is their duty to always show affection and kindness to their wives. Men who can't take care of their wives well and make them happy are not fulfilling the duties of their *āśrama*.

Exercise

1. What conceptions do you have about masculinity and femininity from your upbringing, culture, experiences, etc.? Which of these conceptions, if any, do you feel are helpful for your marriage, and which are harmful.
2. What do you think are your spouse's needs? On a scale of 1-10, how well are you fulfilling those needs?

(Note that when you fulfill the needs of your spouse, they are more likely to naturally fulfill your needs.)

Puruṣa Bhāva

When the man misunderstands his role as husband/guru, it is probably because his *puruṣa* nature (the enjoyer and controller consciousness) is overtaking him. This is the potential danger of household life; the association of women tends to excite this enjoying and controlling nature. *Bhakti*, however, is about serving. So a man shouldn't think serving his wife means being controlled by her; rather, he should think of it as his natural position. His predominant roles as a protector and a provider are both servant roles. And what is most important is that service should be done with affection, sensitivity, and understanding.

When there is affection and protection, then a wife will naturally subordinate herself. When there is force and demand, she doesn't respond well; even if it seems to work externally because the wife is dutiful, she won't be happy. If a woman is not happy in her marriage, it usually means the man is doing something wrong. Where there is a happy woman, it generally means she has a good husband.

If a man thinks, "I am the guru of the family, so my wife should simply obey me," it means he wants the master-servant relationship to predominate in his marriage. But since the conjugal and *sakhya* moods predominate in marriage, the obedience he seeks will come naturally as a by-product of a good relationship, just as the disciple naturally wants to serve the guru in reciprocation with the guru's affection. If a husband feels he has the right to force his wife to do things which cause her to be unhappy or put her in difficulty, he doesn't understand his duty. To such husbands, we must ask the question, "Would you be okay with your daughter marrying a man just like you?"

Exercise

1. In what ways do you think you are too controlling or demanding?
2. In what ways do you think you are serving and supporting your spouse?

Earn Your Wife's Affection

It seems that some men care more about being obediently served than having a good relationship. They want their wives to be more like a mother than a wife – to take care of them just because they are the husband. Your mother will happily take care of you even if you don't do anything for her, but wives are not mothers – they will not happily take care of husbands who don't take good care of them. Men should not think that they automatically deserve the affection and service of their wives. They need to earn it by providing not only physical protection but also emotional support.

Exercise

In what ways do you think you can earn more of your spouse's affection?

Make Your Wife Happy

A wife who serves no matter how a man treats her is a special woman. But because she is special, a man may not treat her well because he knows she will obediently serve no matter what. This is a common example of a marriage that continues because of the dutiful wife despite a negligent husband, though the marriage is actually a failure in terms of the relationship. If a man does not make his wife happy, he is setting a bad example of what it means to be a husband and he is failing in his āśrama.

If a man tells a woman that the husband is the guru of the wife, she should ask him what he means by this. It is important that the man clearly understands what his role as guru is. If he misunderstands this, he will likely create an unhappy family life. Anyone who gets married for any other reason than to serve will both be let down and frustrate their spouse.

If a man acts like a real guru, his wife will naturally respect and serve him. If he demands respect without earning it, it will not produce happy results.

Exercise

1. Write down your key takeaways from this chapter.
2. How can you apply these points in your dealings with your spouse (or your dealings with a future spouse)?

CHAPTER 3

A Happy Wife Has a Good Husband

In this chapter, I explain the nature of male and female psychology in order to clarify and expand upon the meaning of Prabhupāda's statement that divorce is usually the woman's fault in a way that will help men be better husbands.

Protect and Provide

If a case of illicit sex between a man and an unmarried woman were brought before Prabhupāda, he never blamed the woman. He said that it is the man's fault, because the man is supposed to be strong and intelligent and that a woman naturally and innocently follows a man.

A man's role is to protect and provide. Protection and exploitation are opposites. So if a woman went along with a man's sexual aggression, Prabhupāda wouldn't blame her. Why? Because the man is supposed to guide her, take care of her, and look out for her. He provides material, emotional, and spiritual security to the woman.

The woman's nature is to follow, and her role is to receive this protection and security. This nature of a woman works well for her when she has a good man to follow – then the marriage is successful. Manu says that when the woman is pleased, the entire home is full of light; or, as we might say today, "When mama ain't happy, nobody's happy!"

To make married life work well, a man must know what it means to be male and a husband, and also understand the inherent nature of a female and wife. Many problems will be avoided if he clearly understands these two things. When a man doesn't properly fulfill his role as a husband, it is often because he is withholding the giving, protection, and emotional support which a woman requires to be satisfied.

Exercise

Has this discussion upgraded your opinions on the roles of men and women, particularly in a marriage? If so, in what ways?

Act Like a Man

A woman wants to be married to a man who acts like a man. Much of a woman's value and self-esteem come from her husband. If he doesn't value her, she will tend to not only feel unloved, but even unworthy. So, when the husband is kind and considerate, she naturally reflects this; and when he is not, it causes her to be upset or sad.

A good husband knows this and thus deals with his wife in ways that support her. Therefore, he is careful to be nice and respectful. In addition, he knows that he must be compassionate and forgiving, and patiently deal with her difficulties and shortcomings. So he tries to be encouraging, appreciative, and uplifting. When he does all this, she naturally reflects his positive attitude and becomes happy and productive. Women want and need their husband's support. That is why a good husband gives his wife what she needs. This is his duty.

That womanly weakness is usually the cause of divorce is an idea that needs to be considered and understood in light of the above realities of male and female roles and natures. Yes, a woman shouldn't be fickle, weak, or intolerant. Even if her husband is critical, condescending, or cold, she should be patient with him. But when Prabhupāda asked his female disciples to tolerate their husbands' limitations, he was certainly not encouraging his male disciples to nurture their own limitations. Moreover, it is much more difficult for a woman to tolerate a bad husband than it is for a real man to tolerate a bad wife. So if a man expects a woman to tolerate his inability to be a real man and his wife is consequently unhappy – or even goes away in some circumstances – he should accept some responsibility for his share of the problem. If she does go away, he should think, "Would this have happened if she were married to a better husband?"

I am not justifying divorce or condoning women who leave their husbands. As Prabhupāda said, divorce doesn't exist in *Manu-saṁhitā* – it is a modern invention. However, we live in modern times and divorce *saṁskāras* are unfortunately alive and well in the hearts of many. Understanding this and knowing how much Prabhupāda did not want divorce to exist in ISKCON, an intelligent husband should ensure that his wife is happy, knowing that an unhappy wife is much more prone to consider divorce.

Be Hard on Yourself and Tolerant of Others

Some men have high expectations of their wives. But it is better that men have high expectations for themselves as husbands, and that they expect much less from their wives than they give to their wives. A good example to follow in this regard is Kardama Muni, who eventually gave to his wife Devahūti all the opulence that she was accustomed to having as a princess.

A strong man should not require the same level of attention that his wife needs. It is nice if he gets it, but his self-esteem is not dependent on it. When a man complains that he doesn't get enough respect, understanding, or encouragement, he is complaining that he is not getting the very things that his wife needs to be happy, stable, and productive. When he is unhappy that he doesn't get these and when he can't be enthusiastic without them, he is not behaving like a man.

Therefore, if the husband is to be the guru of the family, he should give to his wife and children no matter how much or how little they give back in return. When the husband is not enthusiastic to give because he feels that his wife and children are not reciprocating, he is not acting in a male role. (Of course, I am not saying it is okay for a wife to not be respectful to her husband). Wives have a difficult time with husbands who are easily offended or insulted, or who blame their wives for their personal mistakes and failings. Rather than condemn their wives for their own problems, men should pray to guru and Kṛṣṇa to help themselves in becoming strong.

A wise husband realizes that Kṛṣṇa gave him the ability to be more easily satisfied, and to sacrifice personal comforts, conveniences, and desires in a way that is sometimes difficult for women to do. Thus, he can put his wife's needs and desires before his own, knowing that she often needs him to do this. In other words, he does what is required to make her happy, knowing that when she is happy, "the house is bright." To try to make a house bright without making a woman happy doesn't work.

Still, many men don't acknowledge or accept this, even despite the many years of unhappy married life that results from avoiding this reality. However, when a man understands this and serves his wife in this way, she naturally reciprocates in kind.

This is why I have previously made the point that men should not make it difficult for women to be good wives.

Exercise

On a scale of 1-10, how happy do you think your spouse is in your relationship? What can you do to improve it?

Cyavana Muni Is Not Our Role Model

If a man wants to make his wife happy, compliments and appreciation are two of the best ways to do it. At the same time, he must avoid derogatory statements, criticism, and sarcasm. Such toxic behavior puts out the light in household life. A good husband gives encouragement – not criticism – because he knows this is what his wife needs and wants, and this is what will make her happy. Prabhupāda constantly encouraged us, and it gave us life. It works the same way in *gṛhastha* life. If a man feels he will only give honor, respect, and appreciation to his wife if she gives it to him, or if he simply expects to be honored, respected, and appreciated without him giving these back to his wife, then he is not a man in the true sense of the word.

Now, I hear some of you saying, "If what you are saying is true, then you are saying Cyavana Muni is not a real man. And it would follow that Sukanyā, his wife, wouldn't be happy with him."

If you want to get married, or stay happily married, don't have the same disposition as Cyavana Muni. The moral of the story of Sukanyā and Cyavana is not that it is okay to be arrogant or intolerant. The moral is that women should tolerate their husband's faults, not that husbands should demand this of their wives. Of course, if a man is as exalted as Cyavana, it certainly makes it easier for a wife to be submissive and follow him despite his faults. But many men demand that their wives be like Sukanyā without having the exalted nature of Cyavana. If you expect your wife to treat you like a guru, then you will have to act like one.

Change Yourself

Additionally, although women should strive to follow Sukanyā's example, to find a wife of Sukanyā's caliber is rare today. My advice here is meant to deal with the realities that the average man and woman of the modern-day face in creating a peaceful marriage.

Let's say a man's wife falls far short of Sukanyā and he would like her to improve. A smart husband knows that if he wants his wife to change, he will need to change himself. If he tries to change her with his critical words, then he is no longer in the male role of giving support. This shows a lack of sensitivity, and this damages his wife's self-confidence and sense of self-worth. A good husband understands that to change himself, he will need to pray, be self-reflective, and confront personal problems. In other words, he works on himself rather than on her. Just as Prabhupāda said that women need to know how to win over their husbands through service, submission, and a pleasing temperament, men should also know how to win over their wives.

The following story well illustrates how a husband's behavior towards his wife influences her and determines her behavior towards him. The story, although from the Jewish tradition and told by Rabbi Shalom Arush, depicts the interplay between male and female psychology, which remains unchanged across contexts.

I Can't Live Unless My Wife Dies

A rich miser once came to his Rabbi, saying that he wanted his wife to die. The Rabbi was shocked and said: "God forbid. Why?" The man then related his long tale of suffering. He described how cruel his wife was to him, how she humiliated him, tormented him, and maltreated him, to the point that the Rabbi had to agree with him. From the picture the miser painted, he really was living with a monster and not a wife. Once he finished his story, he repeated his request for the Rabbi's help to somehow make his wife die. He said that he simply couldn't carry on living like this.

The Rabbi asked him why he couldn't just get a divorce and then live happily alone. But the man replied that divorce wouldn't be enough for him. He wouldn't be able to relax until he saw her in a grave since she had tormented him so badly. As long as he knew that she was alive in the world, he couldn't have any peace.

The Rabbi asked the rich miser to give him a few days to ponder over the matter and then contact him again. Once the rich man left, the Rabbi prayed to Hashem (God) for guidance.

Hashem enlightened the Rabbi, and he understood that there must be some deficiency in the husband who had driven his wife to act so cruelly to him. The Rabbi decided to send one of his faithful students to the man's home to try to discover what the matter was.

The student, dressed as a beggar, went to the rich man's house with instructions from the Rabbi to enter and search for anything unusual. The student managed to enter at a time when the rich man was out. He heard the man's wife crying and cursing her husband: "That stingy, wicked man. He leaves me here without a penny and goes off to do his business. If only he would say one nice thing to me, but even with words he's stingy. I'm going to make him suffer when he gets home. At least then I won't be the only one suffering."

The student came back to the Rabbi and told him what he had heard. The Rabbi, with this new perspective on the situation, came up with a plan. He called for the rich miser to come to him.

"Yes, Rabbi. Do you have a solution for me?"

"Yes. I remembered the Talmud (a sacred text in Rabbinic Judaism), which says that the punishment for making a vow and not fulfilling it is that one should bury his wife (thus causing his wife to die). For most people this would be a punishment, but in your case it will be the end of your problems. All you have to do is make a vow that you won't fulfill, and your wife will die."

The rich man liked the idea. "Okay. What vow should I make?"

"Well, we don't have a mikvah here in town. (The mikvah, the ritual bath, is one of the most important features of a Jewish community. A mikvah allows for the holiness of a family to be preserved forever.) Why not vow to build us a big mikvah, built to the highest specifications, with every comfort and luxury? It would cost a fortune to actually do it. Don't do it, and she'll die."

"Okay, but how long will this take? Perhaps Hashem will give me a few years to fulfill such a big vow. I haven't got strength to wait that long. I can't bear my wife's cruelty any longer."

"Don't worry. You'll make the vow here in front of me and two other witnesses, which will make it impossible to annul. That, coupled with the fact that Hashem knows fully well that you have no intention of fulfilling it, means that you should get the punishment almost immediately."

"Give me a date, Rabbi. Otherwise I can't take the pressure."

"Fine. I promise you that if you make the vow now, she will die within three weeks from today."

This satisfied the miser. With a joyous heart, he vowed in front of the Rabbi and two others to build a huge mikvah, big enough to cater for the whole community, and built to the highest rabbinical specifications. Then he went home.

"One minute," the Rabbi called to him. "There's one more thing I want you to do."

"Of course, Rabbi. What is it?"

"Well, since your wife has so little time left to live, I want you to put in every effort to make her last few weeks in this world as pleasant as possible. Buy her whatever she likes, give her plenty of money to spend, compliment her, praise her, and generally fuss over her. What do you have to lose? Once she dies, all the money will come back to you anyway. As for the compliments, what do you care? Give them to her now; soon she'll be gone and you'll have peace from her."

"No problem, Rabbi. I'll do all that happily. The very thought that I'll soon be rid of her gives me so much joy that I'll have no problem in altering my normal behavior to make her happy."

Two weeks passed. The rich man burst into the Rabbi's room with tears in his eyes.

"Rabbi! Please! I want to annul my vow."

The Rabbi looked at him and said gravely, "What do you mean? We especially made the vow in a way that it's impossible to annul. Why do you want to annul it? Don't you want your wife to die?"

"That's just it, Rabbi. I don't want her to die anymore. Since I made that vow and then did what you told me – to do everything I could to make her happy – she's completely changed. She's so good to me. She's taking care of me, loves me, and even prays for me. She's become like an angel. Suddenly I realized what a good wife she is, and I don't want to lose her."

"Well, we can't annul the vow now. If you don't want her to die, your only option is to fulfill the vow. You'll really have to build the mikvah, exactly as you promised, with all the trimmings."

With no other choice, the rich miser started that very day to organize the building of the mikvah, and from that time on lived peacefully and lovingly with his wife.

Be a Responsible Householder

The moral of this story is that if a husband acts well, his wife will be happy and satisfied and there will be little disruption in the family. If he doesn't, then most women will have difficulty doing their duties as well as they should. I am not condoning this, just pointing it out as a reality. I fear, therefore, that if we misconstrue Prabhupāda's statements to mean that men rarely have anything to do with their wives' behavior (or rather, misbehavior), we may be inadvertently undermining a man's responsibility in making a marriage work. We know that Prabhupāda asked his men to be responsible householders, and part of that responsibility, aside from remaining married, is to "get yourself married and live peacefully with one woman."

Becoming responsible householders entails understanding that the responsibility of a man is to guide and assist his family in going back to Godhead, like a guru does for his disciples. However, if he can't keep them happy, then there may be no family left to guide.

Unhealthy Paradigms

I am quite concerned, as we all are, about the large number of divorces and unhappy marriages in ISKCON. To this point, the Grihastha Vision Team, in preparing their courses on the *gṛhastha āśrama*, identified unhealthy paradigms prevalent in ISKCON that undermine the stability of healthy marriages.

The negative paradigms they sought to address are in a document on their website entitled "12 Principles for a Successful Kṛṣṇa conscious Marriage." (https://vaisnavafamilyresources.org/wp-content/uploads/2019/08/GVT-brochure_with-crops.pdf). I quote it in part below.

Alignment with Śrīla Prabhupada

- The teachings and example of Śrīla Prabhupada...must be applied with consideration of time, place and circumstance.
- In the field of *gṛhastha* life, one should take into account the local culture without compromising Śrīla Prabhupada's teachings. One should not attempt to simply transpose practices from one culture to another without understanding the principles and values underpinning them.

Spiritual Equality / Material Difference

- Men and women exhibit general physical and psychological differences that need to be acknowledged as practical realities while simultaneously avoiding rigid and/or unhealthy stereotypes.

Positive and Realistic Vision

- One should, as far as possible, avoid both negative attitudes and unrealistic expectations towards married life as both may dampen one's enthusiasm.

If in the name of fidelity to Śrīla Prabhupāda we interpret his instructions in a way that makes it difficult for ISKCON marriages to thrive, then we will be guilty of "the operation was a success, but the patient died." Many negative paradigms regarding women and marriage still abound in ISKCON and are responsible for problems in marriages (I know this well because I regularly counsel devotees facing marital problems). Many devotees have unknowingly accepted these negative paradigms (and even teach them). The work of the Grihastha Vision Team began with the realization that ISKCON imbibed many paradigms about *gṛhastha* life that were causing marriages to fail. The unfortunate reality is that some of these paradigms are still alive and well in the hearts of some, are sometimes being given to us in temple classes, and are still being supported in some regions of ISKCON – all with detrimental effects on marriage.

Exercise

1. Can you identify any unhealthy paradigms around marriage that you currently hold? Why are they unhealthy? What are their consequences?
2. How can you work to dismantle or adjust these unhealthy paradigms?

What Does Prabhupāda Say?

As *kali-yuga* progresses, the number of qualified husbands is decreasing. This is directly affecting the success rate of marriages today. I therefore humbly request men in our movement to understand the grave responsibility you hold to be an ideal *gṛhastha* and how much your example and behavior impact the success or failure of not only your marriage, but also the marriages of others. Prabhupāda asked his male disciples to become "ideal *gṛhasthas*." Had he been of the opinion that failure in the *gṛhastha-āśrama* was only the fault of women, he would have only advised women to be ideal *gṛhasthas*. It is not just your wife's duty to make your family life successful.

"*Kṛṣṇa-conscious, ideal gṛhastha – that, we want.*" (*Śrīla Prabhupāda, quoted in Tamāl Kṛṣṇa Goswami's Diary*)

Finally, Prabhupāda also made this very important point:

"If a husband situated in the mode of goodness can control his wife, who is in passion and ignorance, the woman is benefited. Forgetting her natural inclination for passion and ignorance, the woman becomes obedient and faithful to her husband, who is situated in goodness. Such a life becomes very welcome. The intelligence of the man and woman may then work very nicely together, and they can make a progressive march toward spiritual realization. Otherwise, the husband, coming under the control of the wife, sacrifices his quality of goodness and becomes subservient to the qualities of passion and ignorance. In this way the whole situation becomes polluted." (*Śrīmad-Bhāgavatam* 4.27.1)

This purport shows how a woman who can be prone to deviate and become the cause of divorce is benefitted by the protection of a man in the mode of goodness, because his association will elevate her. Protection is not only physical. The husband, as explained here, protects his wife from succumbing to her lower nature.

Of course, if she acts under the influence of the lower modes of nature, it is her fault; but here, Prabhupāda is stressing that a man, because he is supposed to be more intelligent and sense-controlled, helps elevate his wife by his association.

In addition, Prabhupāda is speaking in the case of women who are specifically in the lower modes. He is not generalizing that all women are. We indeed find women who are in higher modes of nature than their husbands, or than other men. Prabhupāda himself often praised his female disciples as being very intelligent, and he taught us to respect women by saying that the women in our movement are not ordinary women. Men's intense desire to control women through fault-finding, criticizing, and being heavy-handed – no matter what her own conditioning and limitations may be – is not conducive to *bhakti*, neither for the husband nor for the wife.

Conclusion

In conclusion, we need to be careful in stigmatizing women as the main cause of problems in *gṛhastha-āśrama*. We also need to be cautious of automatically equating husbands with the position of guru, because it can have adverse spiritual and material consequences when men are not living up to this role. All of us, men and women, should take personal responsibility for failing in every aspect of our lives. This, of course, is how Prabhupāda trained us all to live.

SECTION SIX

Spiritual Self-Development

CHAPTER 1

How to Change This Year: You Need to Freak Out

Here are some thoughts about New Year's Resolutions. The ideas are simple but powerful, although not always so easy to follow. I have deeply studied the principles behind the ideas and found them immensely helpful. So give this chapter a serious read. It just might help you make some important changes in your life, service, sādhana, or relationships that you haven't yet been able to make.

Our cultural conditioning tells us we should make resolutions for the New Year. Of course, the perennial problem is that most of us haven't followed through on our previous year's resolutions. And it can even get depressing to think about how many times this has happened. So maybe it is better that we don't make any resolutions this year. This way we'll have nothing to lament about in early February when we haven't followed through.

Well, actually I think it's a better idea to understand why we don't follow through on our resolutions, since I doubt that we will ever lose the tendency to want to change things about ourselves and our lives that aren't working well for us. So the important question is, "How do we permanently change our actions?"

It is said that everyone wants to see change in others and the world, but nobody wants to change themselves. Why? Because it is difficult and uncomfortable. It seems easier to keep the status quo, even if the status quo is less than desirable.

How Kṛṣṇa Gets Us to Change

The secret to change is to understand the process Kṛṣṇa uses to change people and then willingly apply this process on ourselves. So how does He do it? Before I answer this question I would like to ask you to think about a time you changed something in your life. What caused you to change?

Next, think about something you told yourself you would change and never followed through on.

Herein lies the answer to change.

We change when we have to, either to survive, to prevent ourselves from extreme distress, or when we are really sick and tired of something in our life that we just can't tolerate anymore. And we normally don't change, even when we want to, when the above conditions are absent (unless, of course, someone is forcing us to change and making our lives miserable if we don't, which is really a nuance of the same principle: we don't change when we see the light, we change when we feel the heat).

Before I reveal the simple open secret Kṛṣṇa uses and how we can personally apply it in our lives, we first must acknowledge that there are many things in our lives we have the power to change: our *sādhana*, relationships, health, abilities, or level of success, to name just a few.

But when does the change actually take place? We change when we make the decision that, "I have had enough, I must change." If there is something we don't change that we could change, then we need to acknowledge that we are deciding that changing is more painful than leaving things as is.

It is important to mention here that there are many more things we can change than we are willing to admit. Once we stop blaming others or situations for our shortcomings, it becomes clear that not changing is a choice to keep the status quo – which, of course, might be rooted in a belief that this is just the way I am. Anyway, no matter who you are, you can always be a better version of yourself.

Enough Is Enough!

Even though we resist change, in most cases not changing is actually more painful than changing. But how do we face this reality? Stare this reality straight in its face. Don't run from problems. Embrace them and work on them.

Focus on the bad results you are getting from actions or attitudes you really need to change. Then ask yourself this question: If I don't change _____________ (fill in the behavior) then in ten years when I am still reaping the same negative results, how will I feel? Does this thought freak you out and make you feel miserable? It should. If it doesn't, replace the words "ten years" with "when I am an old man or woman." The point is that you need to associate enough pain with undesirable behavior that it motivates you to change.

If not, keep meditating on it until it does! This is the key to change. Our present circumstances (which are caused by the behavior we need to change) have to become intolerable to us. If they are not, our efforts to change will fail. We will still be okay with how things are.

"Okay" is really the enemy.

If you actually allow yourself to deeply meditate on this question, and allow yourself to feel the discomfort of answering the question, it can be powerful. Because until you say "I have had it" you probably will opt for the pain of continuing to not achieve the results and changes you need in exchange for experiencing the perceived "lesser pain" of not changing.

How can I say this? I have changed things in my life that were extremely difficult for me to change; some actions and ways of thinking that I felt were wired to my nature. But living with the results year in and year out made life so unpleasant that one day I said, "That's it!"

In some cases it took me decades to come to this point.

I have seen people at *Japa* Retreats say "That's it" about bad *japa*. In fact, if they don't say this, they tend to eventually default to the bad habits they had before they came to the retreat. We can apply this principle to our service, marriage, finances, etc. As long as we are okay with "okay" we won't change. Why? Because we won't need to. Until we are no longer okay with "okay *japa*," an "okay marriage," "okay *sādhana*," "okay service," an "okay financial situation," etc. we won't be impelled to change.

The point is this: resolutions must be goals connected with deep seeded needs to change. When the "I should" becomes "I must," then we will change. At this point we will commit until we succeed.

And this is exactly how Kṛṣṇa helps us become Kṛṣṇa conscious. When we hit dead ends in our lives and the walls close in on us, we have to act differently. It is discomfort which moves us into different ways of thinking, being, and acting. And when we act differently, we get different results. We can't change by knowing we need to change; we change by acting differently. As long as we continue to act the way we always have, no amount of knowledge not acted upon will change anything in our lives (other than enable us to give some good lectures on how to change LOL!)

The Pain of Past Activities

Patañjali writes in the *Yoga Sūtras* that attachment arises from remembering past pleasant activities. As we remember the pleasure of these activities we become attached to doing them again. Detachment works in a similar way: we remember the pain of past activities and we detach from them. If your brain links pain with activity in the past, as well as with doing that activity in the present and the future, you will give it up. It then becomes a neural response because you feel the pain in your nervous system. It is no longer information; you simply can't act that way again.

We have often heard that it is said that we don't really believe that material life and the material world is that bad, for if we did we would be completely surrendered. But we know the material world cannot satisfy us. This is why we became devotees. So, why are we still attached? It is because the conviction is only in our minds, not in our nervous system, not on the gut level where we look at an activity and say, "That would be so painful that I could never do that again."

So if you want to make a resolution for this year, you will need to associate so much pain with not following through that there will be no other option than to do it. This is how Kṛṣṇa brought us to Kṛṣṇa consciousness, and this is how Arjuna became Kṛṣṇa conscious. Using this same process, we can make resolutions that we can actually follow through on.

CHAPTER 2

Don't Die With Your Music in You

Devotees often ask me, "How do I know my nature and how do I find my inspiration?"

This chapter offers ways to answer this question.

Magic Wand

If you had a magic wand and could change anything, what would you want to change (what problem or problems would you want to solve)?

Would you love to see:

- The divorce rate in ISKCON drop to zero;
- Devotees only drinking milk from protected cows;
- Devotees earning a living by promoting Kṛṣṇa consciousness;
- Devotees living together in huge rural communities;
- Animal slaughter made illegal;
- Kṛṣṇa conscious orphanages around the world?

What problem in ISKCON – or the world – would you like to see solved?

By isolating where you would wave your magic wand, you may discover services that would be inspiring for you, services that perhaps you could dedicate your entire life to. In other words, where there is a problem there is also a service – a service to solve the problems. And when you continually notice the same problem, it just might mean Kṛṣṇa is choosing you to do something about it.

What Bothers You?

Does it bother you that books are not published in a certain obscure language, a center doesn't exist in a specific location, or that an educational program to train men and women to be excellent husbands and wives doesn't exist in your city? Do you feel bad that a traveling theater troupe doesn't exist in your country or are you concerned that there are so few Bhakti Centers and loft programs? Does it bother you to see devotees working long hours in ordinary jobs when we could create devotee-owned businesses?

Is there something that weighs heavy on you, perhaps so heavy that you don't feel you can peacefully leave the world until the situation is being addressed?

Maybe Kṛṣṇa is making you see these things because you are meant to do something about them.

Do you ever think:

- "Why does it have to be like this?"
- "It would be really wonderful if ..."
- "My pet peeve is that ..."
- "Why aren't any devotees thinking about ..."
- "Why aren't any devotees doing ..."

These are more indications of where you can serve. But sometimes you fall into the trap of complaining about the problems rather than solving them. This is unfortunate. If you complain, you're acknowledging that something better exists but are not willing to take responsibility to create it. It is better to see every problem as a potential mission calling you to action in Prabhupāda's service.

With a goal to serve, let's ask ourselves questions like:

- What am I really passionate about?
- What really upsets me that I want to change?
- What do I dream about doing or changing?

What's Your Mission?

Why is mission so important? If you are not very inspired, it is likely that you don't have an inspiring mission or goal.

You can't do everything. You need to focus on one or two things that inspire you, and then become really good at what you do. And if you do something you love, you will find it natural to give your energy and time to it. If you are not working in your dharma, just thinking about your work can bore you – even put you to sleep.

What Excites You?

- What do you love to do?
- If money were not an object, what would you do?
- If you could do anything, what would it be?
- How do you want to help people?
- What change in the world do you want to make?
- What did you love to do as a child?

And here is an interesting thought: if you found out you only had a few weeks to live, what would you regret not having done (or not having finished)?

Is there a book in your heart that needs to come out? Is there a project, group, workshop, or organization living inside you that needs to be created?

What do you dream about doing?

The World Is Waiting

There are many people waiting for you to fulfill your mission because they will benefit from it. You don't know them, but know for sure they are out there.

- What problem in the world have I been created to solve?
- Which group of people have I been sent to serve?
- What change in the world have I been designed to make?

Maybe you are just meant to serve others and help them in their mission. Maybe you are meant to organize, to cook, to clean, to advise, to manage, to create, or to destroy. Whatever it is, don't die with your music in you.

The world is waiting for you.

CHAPTER 3

Humility Means Happy Small

In this chapter, I relate a conversation I had with a godbrother about the relationship between power, self-confidence, self-esteem, submissiveness, and humility. He was preparing a course on humility and asked me some questions.

How to separate personality from humility? Can a strong person be humble?

I see two distinct aspects of humility: dependence on Kṛṣṇa and acknowledging one's faults. A strong personality may be better at the former and have more trouble with the latter.

But there are healthy and unhealthy ways of being strong. So depending on how balanced a person is, they could also at least act humbly, even if they tend to be domineering by nature. If they work on themselves, they could also restrain their critical side.

There is a saying that it is often easier to act your way into a new way of thinking, than to think your way into a new way of acting. The path to humility is paved with the practice of humility, a practice that is done long before humility arises in our hearts. Isn't this how cultured people act even though they may not be naturally humble?

The key is that we see humility as something special, as a most desirable goal. And we should be aware of our own lack of humility.

In my course on humility we ask, "What do you want people to believe about you?" It brings attention to how we try to impress people. We also ask:

- Why is it important for people to believe this about you?
- What do you doubt in yourself, that you need people to believe this about you?
- Who specifically do you need to believe this about you?

A humble person is submissive. Can a submissive person be proud? Can a proud person be submissive?

I am proud to be a disciple of Śrīla Prabhupāda. So there is a transcendental aspect of pride, one that has no ego in it. I know that if I am advancing, I will become more humble. So I must be able to monitor humility in myself. But I should monitor this objectively, without being proud. This can be done, and I believe it needs to be done. I can test whether or not I am becoming more humble, while remaining humble enough to not be proud of my advancement.

Regarding being proud and submissive, we saw that proud devotees were submissive to Śrīla Prabhupāda. Those who are not naturally humble can be submissive to those they greatly respect. But since a proud person tends to think himself more intelligent than others, he will find it difficult to submit to most people.

I define humility as "happy small" and lack of self-esteem as "unhappy small." Do you agree?

Yes. We can be happy being small and insignificant. But one who lacks self-esteem generally finds this difficult as they need recognition.

A human's greatest need is to be appreciated. So, on the human level, this is where we are at. And this doesn't have to be so bad. But when the need is abnormal, there will be problems. Those who lack self-esteem tend to be self-centered, even neurotic, and are often jealous and envious of others. They are often easily offended and complain a lot about others. So low self-esteem can cause many problems. However, self-esteem problems are not necessarily a consequence of spiritual weakness.

A healthy attitude is to be dissatisfied with yourself and strive for the ideal. How is that different from a lack of self-esteem?

I would say a better outlook is to be satisfied with where you are at, but strive to be better. By satisfied I mean accept where you are at and focus on where you want to go. Where you are looking to go is more important than where you presently stand.

If we use your definition above, we find that if one lacks self-esteem one will usually not strive for high ideals. This is because they won't feel worthy of those goals, or they will lack the self-confidence needed to achieve those goals. Devotees often have very low spiritual goals. It can be partially due to not feeling that Kṛṣṇa really cares about them. Or it may be that they don't really care much about themselves.

A bad attitude is being satisfied with oneself and not striving for the ideal. How is this different from healthy self-esteem?

What you describe is *tamo-guṇa*. If you are not striving to move forward, then being satisfied keeps you down.

My understanding of healthy self-esteem is that you think you are lovable and worthy of success, and that you don't deny what's good about you. If you are not striving to improve yourself in some way, you might lack self-esteem because you don't think you deserve better. If you are satisfied in goodness, you won't be lazy. You will be satisfied with whatever you achieve, but it doesn't mean you won't try to be the best you can be in all that you do.

Can a person with low self-esteem be spiritually advanced? Can a person with healthy self-esteem not be spiritually advanced? Is there an absolute correlation between the two?

Yes, to the first two questions. But if one has low self-esteem, it can be an impediment because of the need to pull others down. Of course, high self-esteem doesn't guarantee spiritual advancement, but generally such persons have an easier time confronting and dealing with their faults.

I find that many of the devotees' problems come from not loving themselves, that is, they neglect their *sādhana* because they don't care enough about themselves to be strict. Also, they may offend devotees, not always because of spiritual weakness, but because of negative psychological factors.

Do you agree with the statement, "Humility is to be happy feeling oneself small"?

I sometimes define humility as, "The happiness of feeling insignificant". Otherwise, if we can't be happy being small, we become envious when others are bigger than us.

Śrīla Bhaktisiddhānta Sarasvatī Thakura said, "The reason I find fault is that I am proud." He didn't say it is because I am smart and thus can see the fault. He said that we should not find fault even if objectively there is a fault (unless it is your service to point out another's faults). To demonstrate this he once praised a devotee who wasn't chanting his rounds by saying, "If I didn't chant my rounds I would have fallen down, but this devotee is doing service all day even though he is not chanting. Just see how his heart is overflowing with *bhakti*!"

Would you agree with this analysis? Highest consciousness: Being "happy small" and happy with who we are, despite our shortcomings.

Yes, we really need to be happy with who we are and where we are at in our Kṛṣṇa consciousness. In the Bible it says if one criticizes you, take it as a pearl, as something of value, because you can now improve yourself. If we are reluctant to look at our faults or have others point them out to us, we prevent ourselves from improving. So a humble person is happy to find out how to improve.

Unfortunately, in spiritual circles, it is not uncommon for people to become proud because of the high honor given to them.

Highest: Being happy small, being secure in what we are, and not lamenting for what we are not.

Lowest: Not being happy small, wanting to be great (ego), condemning oneself, and being jealous or envious of others.

Yes, and rather than highest and lowest, I see this more as healthy and unhealthy.

To what extent is a lack of self-esteem a spiritual problem and to what extent is it a psychological one?

In most cases it is a material/psychological problem, which may or may not be solved spiritually, depending on the severity of the problem and the nature of the individual.

It will be a spiritually-based problem when one misunderstands humility and tries to feel himself to be like a worm in stool, not understanding that such thoughts are a by-product of love of Kṛṣṇa. Of course, you have to answer this question on a case by case basis, but I am seeing that often the problems devotees face are psychological rather than spiritual.

What is your definition of humility that covers all bases?

In my teaching on the topic, I came to some basic realizations about humility:

1. Dependence on Kṛṣṇa, meaning I am not the doer. If I think in this way, I inherently feel like Kṛṣṇa can have confidence to put people's lives in my hands, because I know that my power comes from Him. If I don't think this way, He won't trust me – and He might even kick me out!
2. A desire and willingness to see my faults, either by my own introspection or from others' inputs. This also means not focusing on others' faults. If I focus on improving myself, and I have a willingness to admit my faults, then I lose the need to focus on others' faults, which, of course, harms me.

Another point is that we often criticize and belittle ourselves out of pride, because we want to send a message that no one else has to criticize us. Since we are afraid of hearing criticism of ourselves by others, we send out a message that basically says, "I already know how bad I am, so you don't have to tell me."

CHAPTER 4

What Is the Problem

Are you properly dealing with problems that negatively impact your bhakti?

I have often neglected to wholeheartedly deal with my personal problems and I can testify that they rarely go away on their own. But when I step back, look at how they affect me, and make a concerted effort to deal with them, I am amazed at how much easier it becomes to deal with those so-called big problems.

The purpose of this chapter is to get you to deal with issues that are negatively impacting your spiritual life. In doing so, we also look at what might be holding you back from fully confronting them.

What's Your Problem?

The problem, Prabhupada said, is that we all want to be God. Okay, we know that's the problem, but specifically how does that manifest for you? What are the biggest obstacles on your path? What are the biggest things standing between you and Kṛṣṇa?

If we are to make steady advancement, we need to confront and deal with our problems on a regular basis. Are you doing that? Unfortunately, too many of us aren't.

People get into trouble when they ignore their problems. For example, people get into financial trouble when they ignore their financial realities. They spend more than they earn, but either don't want to admit it or don't realize they are doing it. These "avoiders" don't like to get into the details of their financial situation. And this usually causes them to go into debt.

A similar phenomenon happens in relationships. A relationship is not going well, but one partner doesn't want to admit it. "No, we get along well. Everything is fine." Yet, the wife is unhappy and might even be thinking of divorce. She wants to directly deal with issues that are upsetting her but she can't convince her husband to talk about them. He's either oblivious to the problems or afraid to admit there are any. Often, he just thinks it's a personal issue his wife needs to work on. Then one day he gets shocked into realizing how big the problem actually is when his wife tells him she is divorcing him.

Are you doing something similar with your spiritual problems?

How Kṛṣṇa Conscious Would You Be?

To help motivate you to deal with the biggest obstacles you face in your spiritual life, I want you to imagine what your Kṛṣṇa consciousness would be like if those problems were no longer obstacles for you – or if they didn't exist at all? How much better off would you be? How much easier would it be to become Kṛṣṇa conscious? How much more inspired would you be? How much happier would you be? And how much more Kṛṣṇa conscious would you be?

Why?

If you are not facing your problems and doing something about them, it's important to ask yourself why. Maybe you are afraid to face them. Maybe you simply don't want to bother because it's distasteful. Perhaps you think it's going to be too difficult. Maybe you think you can't overcome them. Or maybe you are not aware of them.

Whatever the reason, Cāṇakya Paṇḍita says: Don't neglect to immediately deal with disease, fire, and debt. This holds true with diseases of the heart.

Festering Problems

There is another reason you might not be fully dealing with your problems: you think if you just chant Hare Kṛṣṇa and continue with your devotional practices, the problems will go away. If you have been chanting and practicing *sādhana* for a while and you still have problems that distract you from Kṛṣṇa, it may be that your practice is not steady or the quality of your practice is not high.

You might ask, "Won't I eventually overcome all my problems if I keep chanting and apply the process?" Yes and no. Yes, if you are careful to weed out your *anarthas*, practice sufficient levels of detachment, and have strong and steady *sādhana*. And no if you don't. I've seen many devotees become weak while doing little or nothing to work on their problems. It's all too common. This is why I am asking you to isolate your biggest obstacles and do something about them.

We all need to do more than just hope the problem will eventually go away. Of course, hope and prayer is part of the solution. But as I've often said, pray like it depends on God and act like it depends on you.

A Vicious Cycle

"But aren't these *anarthas* there because of my conditioning? And can I really do something about them? Won't they just gradually go away as I advance in Kṛṣṇa consciousness?" Again, the answer is yes and no.

If you don't do something about them, two things might happen: you might not be in Kṛṣṇa consciousness in the future to do something about them, or they may have such a detrimental effect on your Kṛṣṇa consciousness that your *sādhana* may become weakened to such a degree that it may not be effective in uprooting your *anarthas*. Pulling the weeds out of your devotional garden is a part of *sādhana* that many of us neglect. And we are especially prone to neglect this when we are spiritually weak. It's a vicious cycle that must be broken.

In the purport to *Śrīmad-Bhāgavatam* 2.2.30, Prabhupāda explains, "The devotee must therefore be very careful to uproot the different weeds in the very beginning. Only then will the healthy growth of the main creeper not be stunted."

What Are You Pretending Not to Know?

As I mentioned, one reason we might not deal with a problem is that we are afraid to admit we have it. For example, there are plenty of people who steadily hold jobs and support their families, but at the same time drink a little too much alcohol every evening. Although such people are actually alcoholics, they either don't realize it or can't face admitting it. So look a little deeper for problems that are less apparent.

If you haven't yet isolated your problems, please do that now. Take a good objective look at what you are up against – what is holding you back from being more Kṛṣṇa conscious.

Don't Hesitate

If you are hesitant to do this, know that it's much more difficult to live with problems and obstacles than it is to deal with them. So if you fear facing your problems because you think it's going to be difficult, or you think you might fail, you'll be much better off in the future if you start seriously working on them now.

Struggling year after year with obstacles that are holding you down is much more painful and difficult than doing the work to uproot them.

What's Your Excuse?

Now that you have noted what you will seriously deal with, it's time to look at your excuses for not taking full responsibility to deal with these problems. The following exercise will help you isolate your excuses. And it may also make you aware of problems you haven't yet noted.

Isolate each of your problems and then write down the excuses you make for either not dealing with them at all or as well as you should. These can be excuses you make to someone else or excuses you make to yourself. While doing this, look for possible excuses that are so subtle that you are not even aware you are making them.

Here are some examples of why people don't deal with their problems. This will help you get started on your list.

- It's okay, everyone has this problem. I am just human.
- This is just the way I am. I can't change.
- I never realized how much this problem affects me.
- I never realized this was actually a problem.
- I never cared enough to do anything about it.
- I gave up on it years ago after it kept reoccurring.
- I just figured it would eventually go away.
- I didn't know how to deal with it.
- I just don't think about it.

Can You See How Each Excuse Energizes and Strengthens the Problem?

Write down each of your biggest problems, obstacles, *anarthas*, or weeds in the heart, and under them write down the excuses you make for not fully taking responsibility to overcome them.

Or you can write it the following way, and this might help you see a few other problems you need to deal with.

- When I … it's because …
- When I am … it's because …
- When I do … it's because …
- When I don't … it's because …
- When I get … it's because …
- I am not making steady advancement because …
- I don't have enough … because …
- I have not taken time to … because …
- I have not paid enough attention to … because …
- I have not put an end to my bad habit of … because …
- My failures are usually because of …

Excuses Are Losing Ideas

As long as you think you have a good excuse, you'll have no reason to change. Read this list and admit that you need to take responsibility for these problems. Excuses are losing ideas. Your problems are your fault – **and your success is your fault also.**

"Liberty means responsibility. That is why most men dread it." (George Bernard Shaw)

Did you do the exercises? If not, maybe your ego is fighting back. Maybe your ego can't handle admitting you are not as great as you think you are. Maybe you are having trouble dealing with the fact that you are not as great as you want others to think you are. I've been there, and done all that. But consider this: you might be thinking this way because **you like feeling spiritual more than you like being spiritual**. I know for myself that it's hard to admit I am not as Kṛṣṇa conscious as I or others think I am.

The Excuse for the Excuse

If you haven't done the exercise, at least write down your excuse for not writing down your excuses.

I want to make it clear what these excuses really mean. So after each excuse, I would like you to either write "to go back to Godhead" or "to improve my relationship with Kṛṣṇa" (or something similar that is appropriate for you). For example, if your excuse is, "I don't want to take the trouble," it will now read, "I don't want to take the trouble to go back to Godhead" or "I don't want to take the trouble to improve my relationship with Kṛṣṇa."

Now look at your excuses again (either from the exercise or at your excuses for not doing the exercise), and ask yourself this: "Am I going to let these dumb excuses get in the way of my relationship with Kṛṣṇa?"

You see, your problems are not the real problem. Your excuses are the real problem.

CHAPTER 5

Taking Responsibility Is Liberating

In this chapter, we talk about responsibility. Responsibility means the ability to respond to a problem with a solution rather than with blaming.

There's a story that once Prabhupāda found a painting that was sitting on the ground and he asked his servant who put it on the ground, to which the servant replied that he didn't know, it was not his responsibility. Prabhupāda said, "It is too your responsibility." In other words, Prabhupāda said that when we see something wrong in a temple, we should think that it is our responsibility that the problem exists and we should therefore do what we can to remedy the situation.

By taking more responsibility for our lives, we become more successful. Although taking full responsibility for everything we have done in the past, do in the present, and will do in the future might seem like a burden, it actually brings freedom and inner peace. How is this? By taking responsibility we no longer make others responsible for our happiness or success. Instead, we take responsibility for our own activities and results. We do not give reasons why we can't do something; instead, we concentrate on what we can do.

In the past, disturbances in some places in ISKCON caused many devotees to leave the movement. Naturally, many of the devotees who remained were discouraged, and thus a lot of their energy was spent on thinking how bad things were. A more responsible attitude would have been to focus on what could be done to improve. As one American president said, "Do what you can, with what you have, right where you are."

Recognizing the harmful effects of blaming and complaining, a church came up with a "no-complaining" campaign that transformed their community. Complaining is like digging your own grave because with each complaint you convince yourself you cannot move forward. Complaints are all habits of self-sabotage and it is in our own interest to give them up. Taking responsibility is liberating, whereas complaining is binding.

Turn Off the Victim Mode

No matter how much we feel we are victims, there is always another side to the story. A devotee once told me that her husband had taken money from their joint account, ran off with it, and left her with nothing. This woman was asked by a counselor to tell the same story again, but this time to tell it from the viewpoint that she was responsible for what happened. By telling the story from this perspective, she realized that she was foolish to have trusted her husband with a joint account because past experience showed that he was not trustworthy with their money. This shows that we often believe a problem is outside us when it is really within us.

One way to switch into the responsibility mode is to ask ourselves the right questions. Instead of asking "Why did they..." ask "How can I..."

Another question we can ask when confronted by a difficult situation is, "If I was a world expert on ... (fill in the subject according to the problem – anger, self-control, management, communication) and was guiding someone who had the exact same problem I faced, what would I say to him or her?" The purpose of this question is to gain objectivity in our situation and to make us aware of the options we have in responding to a specific challenge.

To practice reacting to situations from a higher perspective ask yourself, "How would someone who is stronger, or more determined, or more intelligent, or more Kṛṣṇa conscious react to this situation?" Sometimes we think there is only one way to react to a situation, but not everyone reacts the same way to the same situation.

When Taking Responsibility Becomes Overwhelming

Sometimes taking responsibility can be overwhelming. Occasionally, things go wrong all at once and we may not necessarily have the capabilities or qualifications to deal well with the situation. We can take this as an opportunity offered by Kṛṣṇa to learn how to persevere through these difficulties. We can think that Kṛṣṇa is giving us an opportunity to become stronger.

Responsibility also means that when we have little control over a situation, we should act as we would want others to act.

Again, the bottom line is that we should not look at what can't be done, but look at what steps we can take to move forward.

CHAPTER 6

Reasons We Blame or Criticize Others

Why are humans so inclined to criticize? And why is it that after joining ISKCON many of us become more critical of others than we previously were? Considering the plethora of sāstric statements and stories that warn us about the ill effects of criticism, one would think that we would be more cautious about making any critical or derogatory statements about anyone. Still, these warnings don't seem to dissuade us from criticizing others.

So why do we do this even though we know it's harmful? This chapter attempts to answer this question. In my search for answers, I studied our scriptures and the writings of our ācāryas, and since criticism often stems from an unhealthy psychology I also studied what the world of psychology has to say about why we are so inclined to see the bad in others. Interestingly, the explanations of our philosophy and the psychologists are often the same.

In my study of this topic, I discovered 38 reasons why we blame and criticize others, and I share these in this chapter. You'll likely find that some – even many – of these reasons relate to you.

I also discuss the relationship between self-criticism and criticizing others, and the difference between criticism and feedback.

At the end of the chapter, I ask some questions for reflection. These will help you reflect on and put into practice what you have read.

38 Reasons Why You May Be Criticizing Others

1. To make yourself look better you will make someone else look worse.
2. When you see others as competitors you try to minimize them by criticizing them.
3. Your dissatisfaction with who you are (your lack of self-acceptance/self-esteem) results in your being threatened by others' beauty, skill, intelligence, etc.
4. You are reluctant to admit another's high level of success, and to make them appear less successful or incompetent you criticize them.
5. You become intolerant of others' failures (for various reasons) and you believe you can put them in their place, or even make them suffer, by informing others about how and why they failed.
6. You compensate for your low self-esteem with arrogance, and one of the ways it manifests is by asserting your superiority through criticism.
7. You have unfulfilled emotional needs that you expect others to fulfill, and when they don't (or can't) fulfill them, you criticize them.
8. You try to relieve your hurt feelings by blaming others for your feelings ("you make me feel …").
9. Your ego is resistant to seeing or admitting your own mistakes. As such, you focus on others' mistakes, shortcomings, or failures rather than your own.
10. You have a tendency to see the cup half-empty, so you focus more on the bad/faults in others than the good.

11. You see your own faults in others, and because you are not healing them in yourself, you condemn others for having those faults (seeing their faults reminds you of your own faults and the pain that those faults are causing you).
12. You blame others' success (criticize their success) for your failings.
13. You tend to see yourself as a victim and instinctively criticize or condemn the so-called victimizers.
14. You find it difficult to tolerate the words or actions of those who do not conform to your standards.
15. You are critical of those who don't agree with you.
16. You have such a deep need to reform others that you let the world know what is wrong with those who don't live up to the values you believe are absolutely true.
17. You have beliefs that demonize people of other religions, ethnic groups, or countries. Your criticism validates your beliefs and your righteousness.
18. You are frustrated with life and you take it out by criticizing or blaming everyone and everything.
19. You assume others' motives to be selfish or sinister and are thus critical of their actions. (Note that assumptions of others' motives is often a projection of your own motives upon them).
20. You hear or read about the faults of others (we should question why we would want to do this) and it makes you feel righteous and powerful to spread the news.
21. You criticize those who you feel are taking advantage of or exploiting you.
22. You feel life is more unfair to you than it is to others and thus criticize the success of those who seem to have an unfair advantage, or else criticize them for not sharing their advantages with you.

23. You feel entitled to special treatment or status, and when you don't get it you become critical of those who should give it (or who should arrange for it to be given).
24. You have a strong need to be right, which manifests as a strong need to make others wrong.
25. You are trying to get attention or communicate your feelings but you lack the proper skills to do this, and thus the only way to get attention is through criticism.
26. You are an expert in a specific area(s) and therefore criticize or condemn others for their ignorance or inability in this area.
27. When you are misunderstood, your frustration manifests as criticism of another's lack of ability or intelligence to understand you.
28. You feel rejected by someone through their words or behavior and you condemn them for rejecting you.
29. Out of revenge, you want to shame or humiliate someone to get even with them.
30. You are frustrated with or angry at a specific family, group, club, organization, or company (or the world) for what you deem as ill or unfair behavior towards you or others, and thus badmouth them.
31. You defend yourself by criticizing those who criticize you.
32. You criticize those who give you good advice you don’t want to (or can’t) follow.
33. You criticize those who have authority in your organization when you deem their actions to be incapable of solving the organization's problems, insensitive to the needs of the organization's members, out of alignment with the organization’s purposes, or lacking insightful thinking and future planning.

34. You criticize those who try to help you because you are in denial that you have the problem or handicap that they are suggesting you work on.
35. You are not appreciated for your hard work, skills, intelligence, or other contributions, and you criticize those whose duty you believe it is to appreciate you (boss, parent, spouse, etc).
36. Another person gets the recognition that you expected (or needed) and you criticize those who gave the recognition or the person who received the recognition.
37. To defend your ego. You criticize because you somehow feel devalued by the behavior or attitude of another person.
38. When people are extremely self-critical, it is extremely rare that they are not critical of others. If you blame yourself a lot for simple mistakes, you probably blame others for the same innocent mistakes.

It is useful to remember that criticism says more about your need to criticize than it does about what may be wrong with another person; it also says a lot about a general predilection you may have to see the bad rather than the good. Strangely, even though we may be highly critical of others, we may never consider this fact.

The Difference Between Criticism and Feedback

People often delude themselves into thinking that they are just giving feedback when they are actually criticizing. So we need to denote the difference. We also need to recognize who may benefit from our feedback, as not everyone is open to feedback.

Criticism focuses on what's wrong with the person, while feedback focuses on how to improve a situation. Just because a person does something wrong doesn't necessarily mean there is something wrong with them. Criticism is an attack on the person, whereas feedback focuses on behavior (children under seven years of age, however, cannot distinguish the difference, so be careful how you deal with them).

Criticism implies that something is the fault of another person. It devalues people, blames them, and usually implies that "I know better." Criticism can also be coercive: "You must do what I say."

Again, feedback is about behavior and how we can make things better, and is diametrically opposed to criticism. Feedback doesn't devalue, but rather encourages us to figure out how to do something better. Criticism blames a person for what they did, whereas feedback focuses on how to make things better in the future. Feedback respects autonomy; criticism seeks control. Feedback is optimistic about finding a solution together. Criticism often comes with punishment for not obeying.

"He who has a heart to help has a right to criticize." (Abraham Lincoln)

It's also important to note that if we give feedback when we are angry or resentful, our feedback will be heard as criticism, no matter how we put it. That's because people will respond more to emotional tone than intention.

Giving feedback in a demeaning or blasphemous mood is often counter-productive because it causes the accused to go into a defensive mood or shut down, often seeing us as the enemy.

However, if our mood is benevolent and courteous and our sole motive is to improve a situation without condemning anyone, we are in the best possible position to help. It also helps by setting an example of a Kṛṣṇa conscious way to solve a problem. Otherwise, when we call another person a crow, we are also acting like a crow.

Fault-Finding Is Autobiographical

Criticism means finding out the faults in others, and humility means finding out the faults in ourselves. Consequently, finding faults in ourselves helps cure the tendency to find faults in others. Criticizing another, unless that person wants us to correct them, will rarely help or change them. But awareness of our own faults is how we change ourselves. Transformation begins with self-awareness. You can't correct a fault you deny you have.

Therefore, it is important to recognize that when we see a fault in others, it is usually autobiographical: it is our own fault, despised by ourselves that we despise seeing in others. We project our faults onto others so we don't have to deal with the pain of seeing those faults in ourselves. Keeping this in mind, we should pay attention to what we can't tolerate in another person, because it's probably something we can't tolerate in ourselves. Likewise, when we are criticized then the other person is likely directing the criticism at a hidden, unwanted part of themselves. My godsister, Arcanā-siddhi devī dāsī, a counselor who, among other things, often helps devotees overcome their tendency towards fault-finding, said this about the nature of fault-finding:

"If you don't have the fault in yourself, then it won't bother you when you see it in others, and instead of being disturbed, you'll feel compassion."

The author Dr. Steven Stosny made an important and insightful comment about fault-finding when he noted,

"'Criticism is the only reliable form of autobiography,' Oscar Wilde said, because it tells you more about the psychology of the critic than the people he or she criticizes. Astute professionals can formulate a viable diagnostic hypothesis just from hearing someone's criticisms."

In other words, rather than arousing the worst in you when you confront another's faults, it will arouse compassion for what they may be going through. As I often say, 'Hurt people hurt people.'

Humility, Low Self-Esteem, and Self-Compassion

If you are a perfectionist, you tend to be intolerant of your own imperfections. Consequently, you tend to be intolerant of the imperfections you find in others. If you are looking to be perfect or to find perfect people, then you are fighting a losing battle; Śrīla Prabhupāda once said to Viṣṇujana Swami: "I have faults and you have faults, so there is no point in focusing on them. This will only disturb our spiritual practice and service."

If you find it difficult to forgive yourself for not being as good – or perfect – as you think you should be, or if you have low self-esteem, then you will need to practice being gentle with yourself when noticing your faults. This means to acknowledge your human weaknesses with understanding and compassion, and to not identify a fault in behavior as a fault in the self. When you do your best to improve yourself, there is nothing more you can do. To beat yourself up for not being better when you are already trying your best makes no sense. Sure, you want to be better, but sometimes improvement comes slowly. And yes, remorse is healthy, but strongly and consistently condemning yourself is actually a tamasic approach to self-improvement and thus an obstacle to bettering yourself. Finding faults in ourselves is needed to create an awareness of what we need to work on. When our doctor finds the cause of our disease, we should be happy he didn't miss it. Similarly, we should be happy to become aware of our problems rather than be depressed that we have them, because now we know what we need to work on.

Changing the Way You See Others

Ultimately, becoming free from criticism is done best by changing the way we see others and the world. When you change the way you see things, the things you see change. When I see you with understanding, you appear much different to me than if I see you with contempt or with prejudices associated with your gender, race, or culture. I relate to you and react emotionally to you based on how I see you, not on who you really are. So if I change how I see you, I change how I feel about you. And if I change how I feel about you, I change how I treat you.

For example, I could adopt the attitude (vision) that all devotees are wonderful because they are trying to serve Kṛṣṇa. With this vision, devotees will all appear much differently to me than if I judge them based on their culture, race, gender, age, position, qualities (or lack thereof), etc. I can appreciate every devotee even if there is nothing else external that I am aware of that is especially appreciable about them.

Vṛndāvana dāsa Ṭhākura writes,

"In order to teach us the absurdity of judging devotees externally according to race, color, family or other considerations, the Supreme Lord arranged for Haridāsa Ṭhākura to take birth in the lowest section of society. All the scriptures emphasize that if a pure devotee appears even in lower social circumstances, he is still to be worshipped by everyone."

Another way to appreciate someone is to appreciate their intentions. The *Bhagavad-gītā* orders us to see devotees who accidentally commit some mistake with appreciation if they regret their mistake and go forward with increased determination. We are meant to see the best in them, not the worst in them – to see them through the vision of their determination to reach their ideals, not through the lens of an accidental setback.

On the other hand, if I have a penchant for finding faults, then others' faults will stand out and I'll become disturbed when I see them – possibly even disgusted and discouraged. Although I see one event, I can see through two different lenses and experience two opposite reactions. Thus, I cause my own suffering when I seek out the faults in others.

There is a *karmic* principle that what we appreciate in others, appreciates in us; and what we fault in others comes to reside in us. Bhaktivinoda Ṭhākura says that we become glorious when we glorify the devotees. It would then follow that we become inglorious when we criticize them. As we know, to criticize doesn't take any special qualification or skill, and we are all quite adept at it. However, to always appreciate another person requires an elevated consciousness and a purified heart.

Conclusion

In the practice of surrender, the first item is to do what is favorable for spiritual advancement and avoid what is unfavorable. Appreciation is favorable and criticism is unfavorable. But I think it is essentially important for us to realize that appreciation can only come from a generous and purified heart. I know it seems that we can be justified in blaming others for our own troubles, but we never see a spiritually advanced person doing this. So it behooves us to go over the 38 reasons why we tend to criticize, note the ones that relate to us, and contemplate how to overcome them.

Once you isolate the attitudes, beliefs and/or behaviors that are causing you to complain, find fault or even condemn others, practice attitudes and behaviors that neutralize this tendency. Catch yourself when you are about to find fault and say something nice instead – or at least don't say anything at all. Ask yourself, "What's going on inside of me that I need to fault or condemn this person?" In other words, "Why am I finding pleasure in something so negative, discouraging, and disturbing?" And lastly, when you see another's behavior you disapprove of, remember Śrīla Prabhupāda's advice that we should act in the way that we would want others to act.

I would like to end with a sobering thought from Śrīla Bhaktisiddhānta Sarasvatī Ṭhākura.

"Even if one is a Vaiṣṇava, if he commits offenses to the holy name, he becomes unfit to render pure devotional service. It may appear that he is still being shown favor by the Lord as he continues to make a show of devotional service without difficulty, the Lord is actually very displeased with him because of his antagonism toward devotees. Therefore, to give up *nāma-aparādha* we must first give up *sādhu-nindā*, finding faults with devotees."

Exercises

If there are causes of your criticisms that are not mentioned above, then list them down.

Go through the entire list of reasons listed above and the ones you just added. Put a check by each reason that relates to you (if you are not certain, or if it rarely relates to you, then don't check it).

Contemplate/analyze what's going on inside of you that is causing you to criticize. Write down your reflections.

What different attitudes, perceptions, or behaviors can you adopt to overcome these causes of criticism and blame?

Write down any realizations, insights, understandings, or epiphanies you got from doing this exercise.

References:

Below are some stories about the consequences of criticizing or offending Vaiṣṇavas that you may wish to read for further elaboration on this subject.

- **Śrīmad-Bhāgavatam 4.2**: Dakṣa Curses Lord Śiva
- **Śrīmad-Bhāgavatam 4.4**: Satī Quits Her Body
- **Śrīmad-Bhāgavatam 6.5**: Nārada Muni Cursed by Prajāpati Dakṣa
- **Śrīmad-Bhāgavatam 9.4**: Ambarīṣa Mahārāja Offended by Durvāsā Muni
- **Śrīmad-Bhāgavatam 10.17.9-12**: Saubhari Muni Offending Garuḍa
- **Śrīmad-Bhāgavatam 10.85.47-50**: Marīci's Six Sons Offending Lord Brahmā for Lusting After His Daughter
- **Śrī Caitanya-caritāmṛta, Ādi-līlā 17.10**: Mother Śacī Offending Advaita Ācārya
- **Śrī Caitanya-caritāmṛta, Antya-līlā 3.3-46**: Dāmodara Paṇḍita Criticizing Śrī Caitanya Mahāprabhu and Other Devotees
- **Śrī Caitanya-caritāmṛta, Antya-līlā 3.99-164**: Haridāsa Ṭhākura and the Liberation of the Prostitute
- **Śrī Caitanya-caritāmṛta, Antya-līlā 3.190-214**: Gopāla Cakravartī Insulting Haridāsa Ṭhākura
- **Śrī Caitanya-caritāmṛta, Antya-līlā 8.18-32**: The Disappearance of Mādhavendra Purī and the *Guru-aparādha* of Rāmacandra Purī
- **Śrī Caitanya-caritāmṛta, Antya-līlā 8.39-100**: Rāmacandra Purī Criticizing Śrī Caitanya Mahāprabhu for Overeating

CHAPTER 7

The Position of Guilt in Spiritual Life

We often fall short of our ideals. Thus, it is not uncommon for us to feel guilty from time to time when we fail to perfectly follow the practices of sādhana. However, guilt can play either a negative or positive role in Kṛṣṇa consciousness, depending on how we deal with it. Is it bad to feel guilty? Can we use guilt as an excuse for falling away from Kṛṣṇa consciousness? Is it right to forgive ourselves, and if so, how do we do this? And isn't it wrong to forgive ourselves if we continue to make the same mistake? These are all important questions to answer and are addressed in this chapter.

When our actions are out of alignment with our values, we feel guilt. When it's too difficult for us to confront the guilt, we suppress it. We do this when we find it difficult to admit that something we are doing or thinking is out of alignment with what we know to be right.

Vedic psychology tells us that the intelligence is activated to process our emotions (in this case guilt) when we fully confront/experience these emotions. Emotions carry information. But if we suppress our emotions, we also suppress the messages they carry. Guilt is telling us that we need to address what is out of alignment in our life. If we allow ourselves to hear the message guilt brings, then guilt will motivate us to improve ourselves. However, if we don't change and simply lament how bad we are, guilt will have a negative effect by keeping us in the mode of ignorance. Thus, we will feel so guilty that we won't do anything to improve ourselves. Chanting with some remorse is recommended by Śrīla Bhaktivinoda Ṭhākura. We can think, "Kṛṣṇa, I have sinned but please forgive me and please help me rectify myself. I am fallen but I want you. Please accept me and purify my heart." This is healthy guilt and it moves us to improve ourselves.

If we make a mistake and then feel guilty, and if this guilt impels us to improve ourselves, this guilt is very much wanted. We forgive ourselves by accepting our conditioning (emotions) and simultaneously working to improve ourselves. We should be kind to ourselves, not beating ourselves up for making a mistake. At the same time, we should get back on our feet and rectify our mistake by ensuring, as best we can, that the mistake will not be made over and over again. In some cases this might mean lowering our personal standards or goals to a level that is more achievable for us at the present time, and from this platform gradually working towards higher standards.

We may fall down from time to time, but as long as we do not remain down, we are not failures. We are failures only if we stay down. It is important to realize that we often only learn by failing. So if we cannot forgive ourselves when we fail, it will have negative repercussions on our advancement. After all, if you learn something valuable through failure, then you really haven't failed. We will not always act in ideal ways, but the important thing is that our vision is set on Kṛṣṇa conscious ideals and that we are determined to reach them despite the obstacles we face on the path. Without a healthy level of self-forgiveness, we may lose our enthusiasm – or even give up our Kṛṣṇa consciousness altogether.

The order of Śrīla Prabhupāda to us is to remain enthusiastic. If Lord Caitanya and Lord Kṛṣṇa are willing to excuse unintentional offenses and sins, then who are we not to forgive ourselves. Lord Caitanya gives mercy to the most undeserving; those who are the most fallen and sinful. The fact that we are so imperfect totally qualifies us for mercy. Śrīla Prabhupāda never rejected any disciple, no matter how fallen, as long as that disciple was willing to serve and continue to make the effort to advance in Kṛṣṇa consciousness.

To remain enthusiastic in Kṛṣṇa consciousness, we need to create the proper balance between self-forgiveness and rectification of our faults. Depending on how we process guilt, it will either be an impetus to advance in Kṛṣṇa consciousness or a cause of keeping us down.

Note

One may ask, "Should I remain self-forgiving even if I continually commit the same mistake?" If you continually commit the same mistake, and if the mistake is a serious one, it would not be correct or healthy to be continually self-forgiving. This could easily lead to blaming unfortunate situations or others for your mistakes, or for not taking your mistakes seriously. In this case, accepting full responsibility for your actions and rectifying your behavior is a necessary means to forgiving yourself. As mentioned before, gradual steps to improvement may be necessary. At least you should be doing something to improve yourself.

CHAPTER 8

Is Forgiveness Possible Before We Are Pure

The Golden Avatāra in this age of Kali, Śrī Caitanya Mahāprabhu, asks us to do kīrtana in a humble state of mind with the tolerance and forgiveness of a tree. This instruction is not meant for the realized souls for they are already humble, tolerant, and forgiving. This instruction is for those who want to become realized souls. This chapter briefly explains how practicing forgiveness gives us the opportunity to practice saintly behavior.

If we think forgiveness is not possible unless we are a saint, it's worth considering whether this might be an excuse for holding onto resentment. We might think, "Since I am not pure I cannot completely forgive, so it's natural to be resentful." Since resentment can be a convenient way to blame someone or something for our personal problems, it's a great scapegoat. It seems like resentment holds onto us and this is what makes it feel "natural". But resentment is not holding on to us; we are holding on to the resentment. Factually, we are keeping our resentment alive. If we stop feeding it, it will die. With spiritual advancement good qualities develop, but our advancement comes through the practice of good qualities before they fully manifest. In other words, the path to forgiveness is paved with the practice of forgiveness.

Practicing forgiveness means not speaking ill of people who have hurt us and not repeatedly telling others how badly we were hurt. Forgiveness offers the opportunity to practice saintly behavior by being kind to those who offend us. In the evolution of our spiritual progress we are meant to come to the point at which we do not wish ill to fall upon anyone, even those who cause us pain.

Śrīla Prabhupāda asked all his disciples, even those very new to Kṛṣṇa consciousness, to cultivate the quality of forgiveness. If it wasn't possible to practice forgiveness, even in the beginning stages of *bhakti*, he wouldn't have asked us to do it. He knew that the practice of forgiveness would lead to genuine forgiveness. This is because it is normally easier to act our way into a new way of thinking and feeling than to think our way into a new way of acting. So if you ever ask yourself, "How can I forgive?" then the answer is, "Just start practicing forgiveness."

Also, forgiveness means to take responsibility for how we feel. So just because we feel resentful doesn't give us the right to act, speak, and think in resentful ways.

Vedic literature is full of stories of forgiveness, compassion, tolerance, and humility. Rather than see these as tales of exceptional souls whose behavior we cannot emulate, we can allow these stories to inspire us to practice the same qualities and attitudes as the great souls. With this inspiration in our heart we will attract the grace needed to genuinely become a forgiving person.

If we are having trouble forgiving, it's likely we are keeping the fire of resentment burning and are unwilling to turn off the flame. The problem is that if we wait till we feel like forgiving, we could be waiting for lifetimes. Better to start the practice today. How? Start by turning off the flame under your pot of resentment.

CHAPTER 9

Self-Compassion

The other day I came across something on the internet about self-compassion. Knowing this to be an important and relevant topic for us, I decided to share my thoughts and reflections on it. I hope this helps you, or at least gives you enough insight into the nature of self-compassion that you can help another devotee who may benefit from being kinder to themselves.

Like ourselves, spiritual practitioners of all traditions have high ideals, and this can cause us to be upset and hard on ourselves when we don't live up to these standards, particularly when we do something (or have thoughts) that go against devotional principles.

When we fail to maintain devotional standards in either thought or action, or even when we desire anything that is not helpful to our *bhakti*, we are usually trying to satisfy a habitual urge or need. Let's look at this more deeply by understanding this phenomenon from the psychological perspective.

When we feel empty, or when we feel we are lacking something in our life, or perhaps when we even feel miserable or sad, we try to fix this emptiness with some kind of gratification. For some it is sex. For others it is alcohol. For many it is overeating or shopping. In any case, we are trying to fill a void in our hearts.

After we do this, we feel guilty because we know we didn't need to do it or shouldn't have done it. So we think, "I am bad because I have no self-control." This then creates a vicious cycle in which we turn to our old habit (food, shopping, illicit sex, and so on) to fill the void that this activity created when we last did it. You go there to feel better, but it only makes the emptiness greater. And the cycle continues. It is a classic description of *rajo-guṇa*, a treadmill of endless unfulfilled desires. It is a perfect system for keeping conditioned souls bound to the material world.

This creates a lot of negativity in our heart. We criticize ourselves. We feel bad, but bad in a way that doesn't solve the problem. As we've already said, the bad we feel creates a vicious cycle, because when we feel bad, we look to drown our sorrows in sense gratification. And it just doesn't work. And we know it. But we do it again. So, of course, we feel bad again.

How do we deal with this?

Acknowledge that you went looking for happiness in the wrong place. Separate your sense of self from your behavior. Then ask yourself, "What need am I trying to meet by doing this?" In other words, why do you want to buy what you don't need, watch the movie you don't need to see, go to that website you don't need (or shouldn't) look at, or do whatever it is that you shouldn't be doing? Are you trying to cope with stress, suppressing anger, avoiding feeling lonely, or running away from something? Or have you given up on yourself and just don't care anymore, so you are not even trying to control your habitual urges? Whatever it is, you need to hone in on what is driving your urge to do or think what you know is wrong.

It's important to be present with your feelings instead of pushing them away. We have a strong tendency to resist the sore areas of our lives, the areas inside that need repairing. We either don't want to look at them, pretend they are not there, or tell ourselves we'll deal with them later, only to put them off indefinitely.

When you see this problem in yourself, what do you do? Many people become more depressed. But this is counterproductive. When you are tempted to slip into a bad habit, you can extend patient compassion to yourself. Understand that you are conditioned, and that this means that you came into this world with an inheritance of negative *saṁskāras* – tendencies for activities that are harmful to you – and also picked up many new bad habits.

Don't beat yourself up. Be patient, kind, and tolerant with yourself. Recognize that you are simply trying to fill an emptiness in your life that exists because you are not more Kṛṣṇa conscious. Then, when confronted with the tendency to do the wrong thing in the future, pull back a little bit and prepare yourself to make a wise, self-supportive choice.

Don't allow yourself to do things which are self-destructive. Treat yourself as you would a small child. Take care of yourself. Nurture yourself. Be kind to yourself. Understand that any actions that take you away from Kṛṣṇa consciousness are self-destructive and demonstrate a lack of self-compassion.

Instead of criticizing yourself, remember that guru and Kṛṣṇa love you – even if you believe you don't deserve their love. Just as they love you, you should also love yourself. If you don't, you'll become your own worst enemy; and you'll prevent yourself from making needed changes in your life.

Affirm that, "I'm changing this behavior because this is how my spiritual master wants me to live. I am changing my behavior because I am meant to live this kind of life." This curbs your inner critic – the voice that tells you what's wrong with you.
Your inner critic holds you down. Although as a guru, Prabhupāda's duty was to criticize his disciples, he rarely did. He always encouraged them. Deal with yourself in the same way. Choose encouraging internal responses to your difficulties. For example, if you're berating yourself for something you did wrong, remind yourself that you are on the path of perfection and that every master was first a disaster. Just be willing to try harder next time.

In the *Manu-saṁhitā* it is stated that a *brāhmaṇa* never berates himself. And we are all practicing brahminical culture. It's okay to not be perfect as long as you keep trying to improve.

When you're struggling to make a change, it's tempting to see your mistakes as evidence that there's something wrong with you. But as Pataṣjali points out in the Yoga-sūtras, everyone struggles on the path to self-transformation. This doesn't mean you should berate yourself every time you get up late, lose your patience, or do something stupid. Rather than saying, "I am so stupid," use a mistake as an opportunity to learn how to not make the mistake again. Self-compassion helps you to do this. Self-hatred makes you give in to such an extent that you won't even try to learn from your mistakes. Instead of improving, your mantra is, "This is just how I am. What's the use in trying?"

Research confirms that self-reflection and self-compassion help you make positive changes, while beating yourself up often turns a minor setback into a major relapse. Not getting up early can turn into, "I can never get up early regularly, so what's the use in trying?" And failing in some way in devotional service can turn into, "I'll never be a good devotee, so why even try?"

This response is so common that researchers have given it a name: the "what-the-hell effect." The problem is not the mistake, but your negative response to it. This tempts you to find comfort in the very things you're trying to stop doing. Or you just give up on a goal so you won't have to feel bad about failing. Studies have shown that in whatever you're trying to do, accepting where you are at and forgiving yourself for past failures makes you more likely to succeed. Why? Because it removes the negativity that would become the very cause of failing.

Having more self-compassion motivates you to try again without triggering the guilt and self-blame that are common when you have difficulty changing. Self-compassion gives you the impetus to think more about your spiritual well-being, even when you're tempted to give in to an old habit. Of course, sometimes feeling really bad about what you have done can make you so disgusted that you want to change. But this change takes place because you feel bad about what you are doing, not bad about yourself for doing it.

What does Kṛṣṇa say in the *Gītā* about not being perfect? He says that actions born of one's nature, even if they are faulty, should not be relinquished. Kṛṣṇa goes on to say that all undertakings are covered by some fault. He is telling us to try our best but to not always expect perfection – that the most important thing is the consciousness with which we do what we do.

The more we perform actions solely for the pleasure of guru and Kṛṣṇa, the more we will get the strength to overcome habitual thoughts and actions geared towards satisfying our senses. As we become more habituated to act only for Kṛṣṇa's pleasure, our tendencies for self-pleasure lose their power over us.

We all need to make changes, because none of us are perfect. Think of the changes you need to make, the big obstacles you need to deal with. Now think of them with self-compassion. As you work to change, you'll be fighting the temptation to give up. Remember that being kind to yourself will give you the strength to change. And never forget that you have an inner resource of wisdom, resilience, and strength: *Paramātmā*. You don't have to fight alone. When you're connected with Him, you will not doubt yourself.

You might find it strange that I would write a chapter on self-love, because self-love seems selfish. My answer is that if lack of self-love was not such a pervasive problem then there would be no need for such a chapter. I find that lack of self-love is often at the heart of bad *sādhana* and general negligence in one's spiritual life. If we don't care enough about ourselves, we won't care enough to uplift ourselves spiritually. So what follows are some ways that we can cultivate a little more care of our own souls.

- Acknowledge that you're worth whatever effort you are making to overcome a bad habit or obstacle. If you weren't worth it, then why would you make the continued effort in the face of difficulties?
- Recognize how you create your own suffering and stress by giving into bad habits (and how you also create suffering by being hard on yourself).
- Acknowledge that neither Kṛṣṇa nor Prabhupāda want you to suffer, that you do not want to suffer either, and that Kṛṣṇa wants you to be happy.
- Allow yourself to experience how bad you feel when you are doing something wrong.
- Out of self-love, begin to detach yourself from doing things that are harmful to you, either in thought or action.
- Don't be artificially humble. Give yourself credit for any actions you take to improve or make changes. Humbly and gratefully celebrate your successes.
- When you fail, remind yourself that you are human, and that failure is both part of learning and a necessary step in making change. Instead of focusing on the failure, reaffirm your goals and focus on them.
- Make one of your goals to become free of self-inflicted suffering.

I have counseled many devotees who struggle with destructive thoughts and actions, particularly with illicit sex. Every one of them tells me that when they go on Yātras and are absorbed in Kṛṣṇa consciousness, sexual thoughts disappear. Why? Because during those times they are fulfilled.

So be really selfish. Fill yourself up with Kṛṣṇa consciousness. As Prabhupāda says, if you love Kṛṣṇa then you are loving yourself. So engaging in pure devotional service is truly the most self-loving thing you can possibly do.

Exercise

To better integrate the points brought up in this chapter, reflect on and write down the answers to the following questions:

- In what ways does a lack of self-compassion manifest in your mentality?
- What thoughts and actions of yours are self-destructive?
- What are you resisting dealing with?
- Make a list of things you can do to be more self-compassionate.
- What do you tell yourself about yourself?
- What needs are you trying to fulfill through self-destructive behaviors?
- Think of kinder ways you can talk to and deal with yourself than berating yourself.

About the Author

Mahatma Das has been serving ISKCON since 1969. He received first and second initiation in 1970 in Los Angeles, California. He has served as temple president and *saṅkīrtana* leader in several temples and has been involved in congregational development and college preaching. He was co-director of the VIHE, Kṛṣṇafest and Bhagavat Life (in the development and facilitation of *japa* retreats).

He now focuses on designing and conducting professionally organized workshops and retreats, both live and online, to assist devotees and non-devotees in their spiritual growth, through his company Sattva (visit www.mahatmadas.com and www.thesattvaway.com). He also counsels devotees and non-devotees, travels half the year, and writes books. He posts a daily video on Facebook. He accepted the service of initiating spiritual master in 2013.

Mahatma Das is well known for his beautiful bhajans and kirtans, both live and recorded (especially for his recording of the *Brahma-Saṁhita*) and is most appreciated for helping devotees practically apply Kṛṣṇa consciousness in their lives.

He presently resides in both Alachua, Florida and Māyāpur, India with his wife Jāhnavā and their daughter Śyāma-maṇḍalī.

He does several online courses weekly on Facebook, and these courses are housed on his YouTube channel and on Soundcloud (you can link to these and his other sites from mahatmadas.com and also sign up there to receive online class notifications). You can also order his books and sign up for online courses on his website.

To connect with Mahatma Das on social media sites, take his online courses, subscribe to his WhatsApp group or receive his newsletters, please go to:

Linktree at **https://linktr.ee/mahat108**